TO! MIKE

[illegible] may
CONTINUE TO BLESS YOU
BOTH.

Over the Wall

A True Story of One Woman's Journey from **Hell** to **Hope**

Over the Wall

A True Story of One Woman's Journey from **Hell** to **Hope**

There is **HOPE**
for anyone, at any time, at any age

Fatima Gould

Audrey Hlembizky

Ronald Gould

TeamsynerG
publishing

OVER THE WALL
A True Story of One Woman's Journey from hell to hope

Fatima Gould. Audrey Hlembizky. Ronald Gould

Copyright ©2017
All rights reserved, including the right to reproduce this work in any form whatsoever, without permission in writing from the publisher, except for brief passages in connection with a review.

Cover design by Audrey Hlembizky and TeamsynerG inc.
Photography by Shondell Brooks

Published and distributed by:
TeamsynerG publishing division of TeamsyerG inc.
Toronto, Ontario, Canada
www.teamsynerg.com   email: info@teamsynerg.com

ISBN 978-0-9952515-0-2

Printed in Canada

This book is dedicated to my children Aldric and Dannelle, as testimony that you can dream big. To my husband Ronald Gould for breathing love into my soul; my family who stood by me. To my spiritual soul sisters Audrey, Simone and Alanna, who empower me every day to love myself and see my life for the miracle it is. And to God, for always showing me that my faith is all I ever need.

Foreword

By Audrey Hlembizky

Dear God, use me...

Yes! I know, for many it could sound a bit crazy. For myself, it is my unspoken truth. My promise and destiny with God. There I was on my knees begging to be freed from the grief and darkness in my heart as I was mourning the death of my late husband. I was held hostage by the fear of not knowing how to support my 7 year old son who was dealing with his own pain. Life hit me hard and I did not have the will to fight back. In that moment I said, "God, please give me the strength to get me through this and I promise I will spend the rest of my life serving you." Since that promise I have served many and through the adventure of writing this book with Fatima, I can confidently say my spirit was not expecting the wave of blessings that sailed into my soul.

I asked to be used and God came knocking with Fatima at my door. Our friendship was certainly not predictable, but our souls were inseparable, and just like the missing pieces of a puzzle, we fit. Writing Fatima's life story fell into my hands and into my heart as an act of divine intervention. This highest power in the universe unleashed a prescription for so many miracles.

Our journey began during a self-development program. There I was, in our class, and called over to coach her. Up until that moment we did not exchange more than 5 words. She was sitting in a chair, leg propped up due to an injury with her knee. She looked up at me, I looked down at her, smiled and said "hello" and she returned that welcome with a snarky "hi." Her face said it all. I was certainly not someone she wanted to have a conversation with. Regardless, we were both there to complete a task. I asked her some questions and she answered. She began to open up and shared a moment from her past with me. I asked several questions and I could begin to hear that she spent most of her life believing she did not need anyone. Just like that, there was a whisper in my ear and I listened. I had no previous knowledge of her past, yet compelled to deliver the message that was echoed in my thoughts. I knew they were not words of my own and I delivered the message, "you were abandoned." She appeared shocked, a slight rage soured in her eyes and quickly shifted to a child like innocence of hurt where she began to cry. That was the beginning of a master plan. A plan greater than who we were. One that neither of us could have ever expected.

Through writing Fatima's story she has become my best friend; my soul sister. Her courage gave me courage and her faith fueled my faith. We cried, we laughed and we grew stronger. She is my prayer warrior and through her love and wisdom I am a better woman. No one could have prepared me for the angle that God sent, through the journey of writing this book, I healed, I loved and my spirituality strengthened. Fatima's life story showed me that the paths we take are chosen for us and at the same time filled with the options to invite our free will to explore.

This book is a tell all tale of one woman's journey from hell to hope. A miraculous interruption in the blood line; a remedy for the generational curses that haunt the soul. Fatima's willingness to share her secrets so that others can give up the shame they carry makes her a hero. She is living her purpose driven life and a true demonstration of faith, freedom and fearlessness. She is one of very few who are so determined to grow and be a greater human being, regardless of their circumstances. Her humor, humbleness and honesty is like a magnet of inspiration and I am certain you will see yourself in her story. A seed was planted in the making of this book with a greater purpose. An intention that was beyond us, one lead by the holy spirit, to be the example for others to be freed up in sharing their own stories so that we can give ourselves permission to fall in love with life.

Most of us spend our lives looking outward to find ourselves. At every moment of difficulty and challenge, in your life, you have a choice; you can oppose your circumstances and fall prey to a victim mentality or you can experience yourself as someone who will not stand down and make a decision to be free. Moving into a space of gratitude and courage allows you to face your walls in life and to not be stopped, to make an agreement with yourself to live a higher life, be willing to be vulnerable and push aside the things you fear. Gratitude is a miracle cure for every moment. It will dissolve the pain of the past and empower you to bring peace to the thoughts that may burden your soul.

There comes a time in life when you know there is a force greater than yourself. When the bruises on your ego no longer hold power, when the pain of your past bares no weight on your heart, when you can no longer live life in the safe zone and a time where there are no more walls to hide behind, but only to climb over. This book has you move through a timeline of pain and purpose, love and hate, and hurt and forgiveness. It allows you to restore the truth of your spirit so that you can see yourself in Fatima's story and be encouraged to share your story too.

Fatima is the light that shines through a dark tunnel and it has been a privilege to have been on this journey with her. From my heart to yours, I invite you to allow your mind and heart to get lost inside the rapture of her indomitable spirit and, at the end, look at the walls in front of you as moments in time, to grow, to heal, to love and to explore so you can declare that **"I AM Over the Wall."**

With love and gratitude,

Audrey

"YOU ARE ONLY CONFINED BY THE WALLS YOU BUILD YOURSELF."

Andrew Murphy

How does one begin to understand who they are? I mean seriously! We are surrounded by self-help junkies, inspirational propaganda, promise driven workshops and retreats. All in an effort to have us look at who we are, why we do what we do and why our lives are like a pot of hot and spicy jambalaya.

There have been times when I was drawn in by the marketing promises of some life altering spiritual destination to go and find myself. Then I would look at my bank account and realise I'd rather be spending my money sitting on my backside in Barbados at Crane Beach! The thought of smelling warm salt water infused air as I suck back unlimited Pina-Coladas while staring down all the eye candy, is all the finding myself I need!!! Fantasizing about a tall, dark, hottie with six-pack abs, who will come and seduce me with a coconut oil massage leading to a sequel of "How Stella got her groove back." The mere thought of Taye Diggs coming to my rescue would certainly inspire me to get my shit together.

The truth is, I was lost and now I'm found. Perhaps the reason we seek words of wisdom from self help gurus is because we are blind to the truth that all of the answers we need already exist within us. There's just too much crap in the way to discover them! We carry around years of pain, regret and anger, while holding forgiveness hostage.

My name is Fatima. I am an ordinary woman who declared, "I want to live an extraordinary life," while still holding onto a truck load of resentment. For the longest time, I believed I was never good enough. I could not turn around my internal conversations from "I can't" to "I can." I was stuck in a self-induced cycle of hardship of just surviving. One that I created, believing that I was thrown into, with no experience or training. I was blind to the warning signs that this view of life can be hazardous. It took me a long time to discover that there is no manual included with this thing we call life. No one is born knowing how to do everything; we simply wake up each morning and take on what the day gives us. For me, I resisted living every step of the way.

I did not get to choose my kinky hair, my big lips or the color of my skin. Just like all of you, I was born into a world of inherited beliefs and stereotypes. Eventually these stereotypes became ingrained in me and I began to think of them as my own. When my life began, I obviously could not have realized that the world had already designed a roll for me; that my future had limits and that miracles would need to happen if I wanted to obtain love and fortune. I didn't choose to be raised by my grandmother. I didn't choose where I lived, who my parents were or how they grew up, nor the way in which the pain of their past would influence their parenting skills. I did not get to choose the political systems that govern the world I was to be raised in or the impact slavery has had on both the descendants of the slaves and the people who they slaved under.

As children we instinctively know love and learn hate. I believe that hate, fear and greed stem from a set of past experiences, collectively rooted in the misuse of cultural and religious beliefs. As a child, I was curious and constantly asking "why, why, why?" My questions were generally ignored or met with disdain and shouting. Yet, that never stopped me from wanting to know the answers. Why I was not allowed to 'knock about' with other kids? Why I'd get a beating if I got home late from school and why no one ever took me to church? I spent most of my life hearing, "why can't you keep ya tail quiet?" and was expected to accept it as easily as breathing.

I, like many of us, was born into what I call a "generational curse." This curse was the hidden road map paving the way in every choice I made. There was a long line of women who came before that handed down their beliefs to me and while they were guided by love, they were also driven by fear. My reality was that it wasn't going to change. I was not in the presence of people who believed I was anything other than a stereotypical hot tempered black woman, doomed to live the rest of her life going from job to job and man to man, on a predestined path of struggle and survival.

I can be a hard nasty bitch. YES, I said it. I'm announcing it for the entire world to hear. For the longest time I've hidden who I am. I blamed my mother, the father of my children and my culture for my shortcomings. I used them as my justification to shut off and shut down.

Finally, succumbing to the circumstances of my life choices and heeding the still soft voice that had been whispering in my ear for years, I heard the voice of God. He gave me the gift of courage and love and for that reason I feel compelled to tell my story; not for fortune or fame, but in the hope that through my story you might see yourself in my experiences and together we can all declare, **"I am over the wall!"**

The Generational Curse

Chapter One

Freedom of choice, what is it anyway? We go through life being asked to choose things and we systematically make a decision based on our current circumstances. Now where is the freedom in that?

Freedom is defined in the dictionary as, "the power or right to act, speak, or think as one wants without hindrance or restraint." Throughout my life I never understood that I had the freedom to choose anything and, unfortunately, I now know what it feels like to have that freedom of choice robbed from you.

We are born and life begins. Until a certain age, we have no memory of our experiences until our first life altering moment that changes how we see life forever. Our childlike innocence gets a wake-up call and we feel like we are watching ourselves through an out of body experience, or in one of those nightmares where we scream yet no one can hear us!

My grandmother, who I call Ma, is the woman who I knew to be my mom. The word 'mother' was the name of a woman who would call every once in awhile and send me clothes and toys from Canada. I had no idea that anything was abnormal about that. All I knew was that I was a happy little kid and Ma was my Ma.

I grew up in Barbados for the first 8 years of my life. It was a life of memories marked by vivid sensations: warm sun, the smell of the hot concrete just before a thunderstorm, the sound of children running around and calm streets full of people living together without fear. My spirit was free and my life was an everyday routine doing the same thing.

One of my earliest memories is of my Uncle Mackie: tall, dark and grinning in the sun. I remember him stopping me in front of the school house on my very first day of class. I was three years old. He knelt down and showed me how to tie my laces so that my shoes stayed snug on my feet. "I don't want the laces to come loose and trip you," I remember him saying in his deep voice. I remember feeling so little and my uncle looking like a giant, yet he took away the anxiousness I had and it made me feel safe.

I'd start the day with Ma's porridge and a hardboiled egg. My lunch was packed in my Peanuts and Snoopy lunch box. I'd get myself ready and off to school I'd go, where I would laugh, be with my friends and be greeted by the line-up of nuns who would check our uniforms, hair, shoes, fingernails and how clean our ears were. I could never figure out what they were looking for, yet all I knew was that they would never find it on me!

I went to a Catholic School ran by nuns. Even though I would get my mouth washed out with soap and get a whipping or two every now and again, school, for me, was fun and the greatest part of my day. It was my time to play and pray. As much as I hated those whippings, I was exposed to God and prayer and my journey with faith began. Every morning started with the Lord's Prayer. Once a week, we would go to the chapel, pray and give our confessions to the statue of the Virgin Mary. I was a little mischievous, at times, so confession was like taking a bath; I could get dirty and know I just needed to give myself a good scrub in the tub to get all clean again.

Ma's house was a 4-bedroom bungalow that was considered to be a large home. My Uncles: Conliffe and Mackie; Aunt Evelyn and my cousins Roy and Toni all lived in our house too. We were considered middle class and we were one of the first households to have running water and electricity. When I was six, I remember watching Muhammad Ali fight Joe Frazier, with half the neighbourhood packed into our living room, 'cause we were the only house with a television.' We had a lot of land filled with chickens, sheep and a huge sugarcane crop. Our house always had a lot of action as my grandmother was a business woman. Ma sold eggs, kerosene oil and sugarcane, which is what paid all the bills. She worked hard and we all worked the business. When I came home from school, the work continued until it was time to go to bed.

I remember asking Ma about my grandfather, as he did not live with us. He'd had an affair and left for America with the other woman, leaving her to raise the children alone. During their marriage, she had thirteen pregnancies, from which nine children were born. One day I did get to meet him once he'd returned, but Ma said he was not himself. The talk around the house was that he'd gone insane. Ma would say, "his mistress set him mad." I always remember my grandmother shouting "I have no use for men!" It was clear she didn't. She was the most self-sufficient woman I knew. She cooked, managed the farm, paid the bills, raised her children, and some of her grandchildren too, all without the help of any man, or really, anyone else. The only memories I have of my grandfather are of him teaching me multiplication tables and how to read… and later, going to visit him in the asylum, or as we say back home, the 'arms house' where they had him committed upon his return from America.

Ma was caring and not very strict. The discipline was left to my Aunts and Uncles. Today, in this society, parents are encouraged not to discipline their kids the way I was back home when I misbehaved: I got lashes with the back of a chair, the belt, the wooden spoon, a switch from a coconut tree and the back of my uncle's hand. My extended family taught me that children were to be seen and not heard and to never talk back to your elders. Most of all, they taught me never to question, just to do as I was told. "You'll get licks," they said, the Bajan term for corporal punishment, left over from the days of slavery in which the whip would "lick" your back, tearing off the skin as it did. Not that I ever got beat quite that bad, but after a couple of ass-whoopings, just the mere use of the word "licks" would cause me to think twice about whatever "bad" thing I was about to do.

As much as these disciplinary measures seem over the top, they were how children were raised in the West Indies and I assume many other parts of the world. As strict as my family could be, all the lashes in the world were worth putting up with because they still managed to take us all to the beach to swim every Sunday.

When I was 6 years old, my great-grandfather died. My only memory of him was as a tall, very dark skinned man who was blind, living in the house my grandmother had grown up in. My great-grandfather was a carpenter and a local preacher, yet as a child, I was never taken to church. I did not understand why? When I asked about going to church, Ma would say, "there are hypocrites in church and I do not want to be anywhere near them. They act one way on Monday to Saturday and holy on Sunday." Ma was well versed in the Bible; she could recite every chapter and word, and yet the only time we would discuss anything around God was when she wanted to encourage us with quotes. "The Lord does not give you more than you can bear," "the Lord would never leave you nor forsake you" and "this is the day the Lord has made so be glad and rejoice in it." I grew up with these words and they were as much a part of me as the hair on my head.

As I look back and reflect on that time in my life, I am able to see how we as children are placed in a box of names and labels, how we identify with ourselves inside the opinions and views of our society. Our community was small and there was so much gossip around my family. I would walk into a room with whispers all around me as people would talk about my mother. At that time, I didn't get it, only knowing the word 'mother' with no specific attachment or understanding of what a mother was supposed to be. Back then I was so resilient that I could create myself however I wanted. I was fitting inside my circumstances, leaving all the significance out of it. Yet, from an early age I was labelled 'not wanted.' I carried it with me throughout my life like the scarlet letter "A" for abandoned. That's what led to most of my life choices and fed my aversion to needing anyone.

***

I was 6 years old when I met my mother for the first time. She came to Barbados to bring my two year old cousin, Toni to live with us. I was excited as my cousin Roy and I had another kid to play with. I recall the excitement of my Aunts and Uncles as they said, "Fatima's mom is coming here!" They were acting like it was some big event and I could not figure out why?

When she arrived we were introduced. I looked up at her and she looked down at me and that was that. All I know is that everyone else was very excited about seeing her and I was told, "this is your mother." As quickly as she came, she left. I recall seeing her appear in my line of sight one more time that day and then she was gone. The next day I was told she went back to Canada. I felt nothing. Why would I? I had no emotional bond, no memories other than a box arriving a few times a year and being told that what was in it was for me.

***

Two years later, before the end of school, Ma sat me down in the kitchen: "Fatima," she said, "you will be going to Canada to visit your mother for the summer."

I listened attentively, with mixed emotions as I was looking forward to a summertime filled with relaxing around the house and going to the beach. I had two thoughts - I do not know this woman and why would my grandmother want to send me to see her?

"Alone?" I asked.

"No," said Ma. "Aunt Evelyn will be taking you. You'll stay there for the summer and then you'll come back home just in time to start at a new private school."

I felt anxious, but at the same time excited to see Canada. It was my birthplace and it could be exciting to visit. Besides, I was going with my aunt. I imagined that I was going on an adventure and would have great stories to tell my cousins and friends about when I returned back to school. When I realized I would be staying with my mother, I did not know what to make of it. My only contact with her were dolls and clothes that I was not even allowed to wear most of the time, as Ma would say, "You only have one back," meaning I could not wear all the clothes at once. She also said, "I had to save them for special occasions," though such events were very few and far between. My Mother did not send me any letters; she would only communicate through my grandmother sending her money to support me every month. At this point, I was told I was going to spend the summer with a woman who I had seen only once in the flesh; who looked down at me with a straight face, put her hand on my shoulder as she said hello and walked away without an ounce of visible emotion. At that age I did not know any better or any different, yet I knew my grandmother and my Aunts and Uncles loved me regardless of how many licks I got. They may not have shown affection in a way people recognize today, but they showed me it in the only way they knew how.

After having spent many years in Canada, in a multicultural society, I've learned a few things about the cultural differences in parenting styles. Nothing ever just happens, there's always history behind how we treat our kids; patterns passed from one generation to the next. Some of these are blessings, others are curses. My generational curse was a characteristic of many black families from Barbados and the West Indies, created during the days of slavery. If you, as a slave, showed too much affection to your children, the slave masters would see this and use that relationship to chastise you if you disobeyed. Children would be taken away, beaten or worse, for acts of disobedience committed by their parents. If a slave boy or girl misbehaved, the slave master himself would often beat or whip them without mercy. The way to survive as a slave parent was to show no emotion and to discipline your own children by your own hand. In effect, the children became no different than property because under slavery, everyone was someone's property.

As a consequence, habits born during these horrible times, found their way into the parenting styles of the slaves' free descendants and still remained hundreds of years later. Unless you really studied, you couldn't have known that was why Bajan parents raised their children as they did. Ask any one of them why and they would say "that's just the way it is."

Ma packed a suitcase for my trip to Canada. Aunt Evelyn was my mother's babysister and was addressed by all of us as "Baby." I loved my Aunt and I have many beautiful memories of her. The most precious one was hiding under the cool, white sheets of her bed, when it would rain, and cuddling. Baby would braid my hair every Sunday, in the evening, and dress me up, sometimes in the clothes that my mother had sent for me to wear, whenever I'd go visit my great grandfather. These visits became the special occasions in which I would have the chance to wear my new clothes. Even though the old man did not say much, it was a great time to get dressed up, get out of the house and inhale the mouth watering smells of baked goods during our traditional Sunday Island meal.

As the days grew closer to our trip, I thought about everything that I loved during our summer vacations that I was going to miss out on. Making mud pies, taking surprise trips to the beach and pretending to play school and house with Roy and Toni. I hadn't even left yet and all I could think about was coming back so that Roy, Toni and I could steal one of Ma's salted pig tails and then using an old tin can and some ground provisions, light a fire and cook some stew. Oh how amazing that tasted! It was oily, but good. Roy also made great kites during the flying season and we would have so much fun running up and down the grass and beach catching them in the breeze. Like Christmas and Easter, Summer vacation was one of the most exciting times of the year.

The day arrived and I lay in my bed with no rush to get ready. I recall for the first time feeling what it was like to not sleep well. I was already missing my bed, yet I told myself that this was going to be an adventure and I would be back soon. Ma and my Aunt kept shouting at me to get ready and come out. There were no smiles on anyone's faces that day; just a silence and the sound of all of us gathering our bags to pack into the car. Ma put her hands on my shoulders and told me to be good. I wrapped my arms around her body and squeezed her tight. She told me "that's enough" and motioned for me to go so that we wouldn't be late. I sat in the car with the windows rolled down and just looked at Ma, Roy and Toni as they waved good bye. I felt sad and anxious, yet when I looked at my Aunt, I felt calm. We drove away headed for Seawall Airport, to catch our plane. During the flight, I had so many things running through my mind. I was mostly thinking about all the stories I had heard of and how cold it was in Canada as there was a lot of ice and snow. The coldest thing I'd ever experienced on my skin so far was when I opened up the fridge to pour a glass of the fresh goat's milk Mr. Leacock brought by daily.

To my surprise when we touched down in Toronto, it was summer, so it wasn't cold, but there was a stickiness to the air. It was pasty on my skin and it made me sweat. This was not what I was expecting at all. The humidity was unlike anything I'd experienced before; the air didn't seem to move, whereas in Barbados we always had trade winds.

As we entered the airport, I was holding my Auntie's hand so tight that my fingers were numb. My head was spinning and I was ready to meet this woman that everyone called my mother.

As I looked around, there were so many white people!!! More than I had ever seen in my whole life. It was busy, loud and there was this voice coming from the ceiling constantly shouting out words. I had never experienced this before. I later figured out that it was a 'PA system.' I was afraid, but I was with my Aunt, so I knew everything would be okay.

We arrived at Customs and before I knew it, a customs officer took my aunt. They pulled me away from her and took me into a small room. The next thing I knew, I heard my name coming from what I thought was the ceiling. "Ms. Devonish, please come to Customs to pick up your daughter Fatima." My heart started racing and I thought, "Where is my aunt? What did they do with her? Why are they calling my mother to come get me? I do not want to see her; I want my aunt back!" I froze and just stared ahead, afraid to move, thinking they might take me away too.

The door opened and there they were. My mother and this man she introduced to me as her boyfriend. We looked at one another for a moment. She said, "Hi," smiled and walked towards me. She grabbed my hand pulling me out of the room and away we walked, back to the general waiting area where we waited patiently for them to release Baby.

We waited for hours. I didn't find out what really happened, in that room, until five years later. As it turned out, my Aunt had been keeping a secret from the family: she had ovarian cancer. Before leaving for Canada, her doctor had given her painkillers to take with her. Customs found the pills and suspected my Aunt for smuggling drugs.

By the time the family found out my Aunt had cancer she was already at Stage 4. I loved her so much! Baby was my favorite. There was nothing miserable about her; not a mean bone in her body. She showed me loved me in so many small ways, the way I imagine a mother would treat a child. She never married or had any children of her own. When she died at the tender age of 32, I realized the reason why she showered me with so much love was that she might have seen me as the daughter that she never had. Baby played a key part in making me the woman that I am today and I am so grateful for having had her in my life, if only for a short time. To this day, I celebrate her birthday on March 15th and her spirit is alive inside me.

My mother, her boyfriend and I sat in dead silence waiting for my Aunt to be released! My feet barely touched the floor and I couldn't help swinging my legs back and forth because I was so nervous! I kept gazing intensely at all the white people. I had never seen so many in my life and I barely saw anyone that looked like me. Here I was sitting beside the woman that everyone said was my mother, feeling nothing. No connection, just an uncomfortable silence, broken only by the pounding of my heart.

Finally, my Aunt emerged and we walked towards her and embraced her. We left the airport to head to my mother's apartment in Cabbagetown. I sat quietly in the back seat after being told to wear my seat belt. I had never used one before! As we started to move and I saw all the cars, it was like being in a movie. My first time on the highway was an experience all in its own.

We spent that summer doing a lot of sightseeing. I met family I didn't know I had. I also met Mother's neighbours. Apparently, they had known me as a baby and would look after me when my mother went to work. I also met my Uncles Addie and Ian whom I had only seen once before. They were Roy and Toni's father's, my mother's brothers. I was also reunited with my Aunt Pam. I knew her because she came with her family to live in Barbados for a short time, then emigrated to Canada to be with the rest of her siblings.

For the most part, my summer vacation visiting Canada was a good one, and my mother seemed to love having me and Baby visit. We went to places like Niagara Falls, took walks in downtown Toronto and shopped at Honest Ed's and Square One. I was also introduced to my godparents who shared many stories and memories of me as a child.

It was the first time I became aware of my infancy years. Who knew that there was life before my time with my grandmother and my family in Barbados? This was all very strange and sometimes confusing. I was also told stories about how my mother had a hard time looking after me on her own, which made it necessary for me to go to Barbados to live with my grandmother.

Stories were shared about my father, whose name was Walter Brewster. He apparently knew about me, would pick me up from the babysitter and would pay for child care. This was, of course, the first time I'd heard any of this.

For the first time in my life, I became aware of the burden of my father's absence. During this visit, he stopped being an idea and became a real person. I had met him once before, after my Aunt saw his picture in the Nation; the national Barbadian newspaper. She called him and he came over to visit. I sat on his knee while he asked me about school. He gave me a red necklace which I kept for many years.

At one point during the visit, my father kept saying that he could not believe that we both had lived in the same country at the same time. Apparently, when he and my mother broke up, she never told him I was sent and was living in Barbados. My parents met in Toronto through a mutual friend and were together for over two years. Years later, my Uncle Addie told me that my dad was the one who got him a job at the CN Rail. Ma had also told me that my parents had been engaged to be married, but when my grandfather went to introduce himself to the Brewsters, Walter's father was very upset that their son; who they had been sent to Canada solely to go to school, had gotten involved with a woman and had a child.

My mother's side of the story was simple. "Your father wanted me to pay for him to go to school," and "I said 'no'." So he found an older woman who already had children and started a relationship with her. "He got married," Mother replied matter-of-factually, "and she ended up paying for his education. They moved to Barbados for several years and had a child together." I learned that my half-sister's name was Lynne and that she was six years younger than me.

This first summer in Canada had some of the most educational moments of my whole life, sometimes in very surprising ways!

"Look at this, Fatima," my mother said, pointing to an important-looking piece of paper. It was a birth certificate and it bore four names – Fatima

Dahne Evelyn Devonish – and a date, August 4th, 1967. "When your grandfather came to visit me in Toronto after you were born, he insisted on all of these names!" she said excitedly.

I looked back down at the certificate. The other striking detail was that my birthday wasn't when I thought it was. How was it possible that I didn't even know my own full name and birthday? These things didn't seem to matter back home. Who cares as long as you have a roof over your head, clothes on your back and food on your plate? You don't need that kind of information to survive and our life in Barbados was all about survival.

In any case, that summer, I spent my actual 8th birthday, in Toronto, with my Canadian family, and though it had been a tremendous experience, in my heart and mind, I started counting down the days until I would head back home to my friends and the life that I knew and loved. I was excited to tell my friends everything I'd seen and learned. Roy and Toni would be amazed to find out the things about our family that I had learned in a single season! I had stories to share about their fathers and how crazy they are, how Ma's children were so much alike, even though they didn't live in the same country… The people I met and interacted with, the food I ate, the sights and sounds of the big city, the crowds and all the white people!

Home was calling me and I couldn't wait to go back.

***

Two days before we were due to leave, I sensed something was off. Baby's bags had been laid out and she was already starting to pack, but mine hadn't been brought out. Everyone seemed a little strange with me and I started getting this sinking feeling in the pit of my stomach.

The day before our departure, I was called into the living room as the sun set outside. I'll never forget it. Baby was sitting in the easy chair to my right and Mother on the couch to my left. Neither of them invited me to sit, though I naturally wanted to stay closer to my Auntie. There was an uneasy atmosphere in the room. Mother was as emotionless as ever. Auntie seemed sad and I was unnerved to notice just how much she resembled Mother in that moment.

"Fatima," said Baby, "your mother and I have been talking and we've made a decision." She looked at me, not unkindly, but straight in the eyes. "You will not be going back with me. You will stay here with your mother."

My heart started racing. I had trouble keeping my breath. "For how long?" I asked. My Mother quickly interjected and said, "This is your home now and you'll live with me. We already have you registered for school in Toronto."

I wanted to scream, shout and cry, but I didn't want to get licks. I did as I was told and kept it in. "Why?" I asked in a quiet voice. Mother responded, not unkindly, but with the characteristic stone-faced expression that I'd come to learn was her normal face. "I've enjoyed having you here," she said, "and now I have the means to raise you myself. It's just how it is."

***

The day arrived and it was one of the saddest days of my life. We drove my Aunt to the airport and I could not believe I was not going with her. It was time to say goodbye ... AGAIN! I hugged her tight and cried on her shoulder. "You'll be fine, girl," she said.

"You know what to do. Ma and I raised you right and your mother will do the same. This is how it should be." She wasn't crying, but by the look in her eyes, you could see how much she was hurting. I was like one of her own and she loved me that way, so it must have been tearing her apart.

My body was trembling, I was so nervous. It was the same feeling as the island being hit with a big tropical storm. In that moment all I wanted to do was hide under the cool white sheets with my Aunt, cuddling and holding each other tight.

There I was, 8 years old, in a strange country, desperate to go back home to my friends and family. As I looked at my Aunt, all I could think about was that I would never again see the big bright sun, never smell the hot concrete, play in the waves on Sundays at the beach or be back in our huge backyard hearing Ma call me in for dinner! It was all lost and I was now left with this woman because they say she's my mother? As I stood there paralyzed with confusion and fear, it felt like someone put their hand over my mouth and would not let me breathe. I felt like I was suffocating. My eyes welled up with tears as I watched my Auntie make her way down to her flight. I remember each movement of her body. Slowly with each step she pulled farther and farther away from me until I watched her disappear.

Just like that, my life changed. I was a prisoner being punished for something that I didn't understand. No one asked me what I wanted. I wasn't given any choice. All I knew for certain was that everyone had lied to me and, in that moment, my life shifted. I found myself in a darker place; abandoned, forced to grow up and survive as a stranger in a strange land.

As the tears rolled down my face, a firm hand took me by my arm. It was Mother. She pulled me back from the line. For the first of many times, anger surged through my blood as she touched me. How dare this woman hold me like that! I felt tremendous rage towards her, a rage that would consume and numb me for most of my life. I felt all alone, confused and betrayed. Why would Ma and my Aunt allow this strange woman to keep me? Why would they give me away? What did I do wrong for them to all hate me this much? I was paralyzed with fear and for the first time in my life, I discovered the feeling of hate.

Shocked by what had just happened, the drive home was like a nightmare. No one said a word as the tears rolled down my face. My lips quivered, my heart raced and my head hurt. I wanted to know where God was and why my Ma gave me away. I had never felt a pain like this before and thought I was going to die. I felt like my childlike innocence was being stripped from me and the scar of betrayal would mark my spirit forever. On that day, I created a blueprint of pain and I was forced to begin a new life: one full of fear, hate and self-doubt - a life where I would never trust anyone again.

Mother

Chapter 2

Therapy. What is it, anyway?

I mean, how do you know when you need therapy? Most of the time we spend our lives blaming others, bad luck or say it just wasn't meant to be. We come to all these conclusions in our minds to justify our actions or outcomes. I probably needed traditional therapy after Aunt Baby left me, and as a result, every day after that 'goodbye' my life became about survival and no longer about living. At a very young age I became a prisoner of my circumstances. I began to form views about people and those views became my shelter and my enemy for the next 41 years.

As I look back and reflect on things that happened, I can see how I made decisions that molded my character, dominated my personality and formed the woman I had become. I now get that we go through life experiencing things, and with every experience, our beliefs alter. It is our beliefs that dictate our actions and those actions dictate our life.

So there I was, 8 years old, living with a stranger named 'Mother' and begging God to send me home every night as I cried myself to sleep. Each day was the same. I struggled to wake up; struggled through my day and I couldn't wait to go to bed- to get under the sheets and cry myself to sleep. I remember always hearing, "a child is to be seen, not heard," so it was easy to just do what I was told and disappear into my sadness. I did not think anyone noticed or even cared.

We lived in downtown Toronto, where there were so many people, especially white skinned folk. I had never seen so many white people. My only experiences of whites back home were some tourists and a hand full of children that went to the Catholic school. I look back now and marvel at how different things are now in Canada. Today, we are a multicultural melting pot, but when I was a kid, my black skin stood out like spilled grape juice on white carpet. I was different and didn't belong and every day throughout my childhood brought new reminders of both.

I was 8 years old, which meant joining a Grade 4 class. Unlike back home, this was a public school so I did not need a uniform. Mother, inherited a lot from Ma. She, too, liked to cook, bake and sew. By that age, I'd grown very tall and most store-bought clothes from places like Willi Wonderful and Honest Ed's didn't fit me at all; they were too short in the arms and legs. Mother would sew my clothes by hand. Even then, it didn't help, as not long after I arrived in Toronto, I went through a growth spurt, so by the time new pants or blouses were finished, I had already outgrown them.

On my first day of school, Mother and I walked into the foyer of the building. The Principal came out to greet us. He was a big white man with a smile that didn't quite reach his eyes. I felt nervous around him, as if he was going to ask to see my passport.

"Welcome, Fatima," he said to me in that clear, formal Canadian accent, "let me show you to your classroom." He took me down the cool, clean hallway to my classroom. The other students had already gathered, mostly white kids: some with blonde hair and blue eyes, others with shades of red hair, and a few Asians. The amount of brown skin and black kids were so few that I could count them on one hand! Which explains the stares I got as we approached the room. With every step I took, a twisty feeling inside me started to swell up and grow stronger. I was suddenly uncomfortable in my own skin. For the first time in my life, I could relate to things they said back home about how my black skin makes me different. At one point, I thought one kid's eyes were going to bulge out of his head! I just looked straight in the eyes of everyone and moved along.

When we entered the room, the bell rang. The noise startled me. It was so loud compared to what I knew back home. The teacher, a tall man with reddish hair, stood at the blackboard,. He smiled a funny smile at me when we entered.

"You must be Fatima," he said. "I'm Mr. Jackson. I understand you came here from the Caribbean?"

I didn't say anything. Mother nudged me with her elbow. "Answer him," she hissed out of the corner of her mouth.

"Yes sir," I replied.

"Wonderful! And such a delightful accent, too! We'll be starting class shortly." Mr. Jackson motioned for me to sit at the back of the classroom.

While Mother and Mr. Jackson spoke quietly, I went and sat at my desk. Somehow Mr. Jackson's comment about my accent made me feel uncomfortable. I guessed that he meant well, judging by his tone, but honestly…what accent? What the hell was he talking about? As far as I was concerned, I was the only one speaking normally.

The first students started to enter the room. They filled up the desks around me, each one of them giving me that same funny look; not unfriendly, but more… curious, like I was some prized goat on display at a farmer's fair.

The first day went well enough, but as I was exiting the school building and walking outside, I spied three girls huddled together, glancing up at me and pointing. That got me mad.

"What's so funny?" I asked firmly.

The three of them laughed. "See? I told you she talked funny," said the lead girl; a blonde I later learned was named Emily Wilson.

"Yeah," chimed in another, a brunette, "say something else for us!"

"You think the way I talk is a joke?" I exclaimed. At that, they just lost it and started cackling like little 8 year old witches.

"Not nearly as funny as your floods!" said the blonde one, catching her breath.

What was she talking about? That's when she pointed and I looked down. Sure enough, the pants that Mother had hemmed for me did not make it all the way down to my ankles. If the basement flooded, I would be dry from the shins up.

I ran back home in tears. I didn't like it here at all! Worst of all, these kids – these white kids – had fulfilled my worst fears about what living here would mean for me. I was different, not special. Worse yet, they thought I was weird, ugly and probably stupid.

Day Two. I got up. My stomach was acidic and filled with anxiety. I went to the bathroom and sat on the toilet. I didn't want to go back to school, but what I wanted didn't matter. It's not like I could tell Mother. My options weren't good. There were two choices: keep my head down every day, being just as scared of girls my own age as I was of my mother or not give them a single gram of satisfaction in their insults and teasing.

Eight year old girls… who did they think they were, anyway? That's when I made my choice. The hell with those little fools.

That day, I walked into school in the floods Mother had made for me. I didn't strut and I didn't show off. The nervousness in my belly was still churning, but I was confident. Emily Wilson saw me again and started to say something. I shot her a look, one that silently said what I wanted to tell her out loud – "shut yuh mouth!" and that look slapped that grin off of Emily's pasty white face.

We all have those pivotal moments where we take an action and voila! We convince ourselves that this is what we need to do to protect ourselves, to avoid being hurt, all in an effort to survive. I planted the seed of defensiveness and resistance to love with the first slap of my look towards Emily. That moment marked the day that I began to believe that the only way to get through life was to intimidate others so they stay the hell away. I convinced myself that this would work and no one was ever going to walk all over me again, at least not at school. Home? Well that wasn't going to be so easy.

After that, those same girls, and other kids too, would try to make fun of me. I would grant them one free shot, and after that, I would attack them back in a way that would send them away crying. I became tough with my words, my looks, and at times, my fists, which became my preferred choice of defence. Oh how I hated school! How I hated these kids! How I hated Canada! And ohhh how I hated Mother!

With each fight I grew angrier, more distant and numb. As the days passed Ma, Baby, Roy and Toni; my friends, the farm and the beach became a heaven that I would have to die to get to. Here I was, was hell!

***

On the fourth day of school, I was walking down the hall to go to the bathroom when I saw her. She was tall. She had papers in her arm, indicating she was a teacher and she looked like me! She was black! I felt a connection, and she must have sensed something too, for she turned around and looked at me. That expression of surprise and delight on her face was something I still remember. Then she spoke, "Hello, I don't think I've met you before. What's your name?"

She spoke like a Canadian. She didn't sound like me at all.

"I'm Fatima Devonish, ma'am," I said, feeling shy all of a sudden.

"Well, Fatima, I am Miss Anita," she said. "I'm a teacher here."

"Are…" I wasn't sure how to ask without being rude, but I had to know. "Are you the only black teacher here?"

Miss Anita nodded no, she was not, and I could see on her face a little flash of something, a familiar expression: that of a misfit. She composed herself and smiled. "I'm glad that you're here," she said. "Now, back to class." I smiled back at her, then turned around and continued the way I was going. A sense of ease came over me and I had my first real smile. Someone who looked like me... who was in a position of authority... was happy I was here! And suddenly, I was too!!!

Before long, the air started getting colder, and we fell into a familiar routine. I would wake up, get dressed, clean up and head to school. Then I'd come straight home after 3 o'clock. I stayed at Marion's home until Mother got home from work. She was one of Mother's good friends and had helped to look after me when I was a baby.

The days became harder. I had never felt air so cold! It made me shake from the inside. All I wanted was the warm sun from home to beam down on me until I fell into a blissful sleep, where I would never wake up. I hated the cold weather just as much as I hated the school and the kids. I was pushed, poked and called "dark chocolate," I was bullied everyday by the same girls as others watched and laughed. I remember thinking what if I found a way to get back home and escape from here? Even if I got in big trouble and got licks with the leather belt every day, it would be better than this. But... I was only 8 years old. How was I going to get back home? I knew I never would and now it was all about being tough. There was no one on my side, no one to protect me. I was on my own and I did not trust anyone.

With each day I was experiencing what it was like to be a black immigrant in Canada. As if school wasn't already bad enough! I was walking back from the corner store, one day, and an white older kid came up to me. This kid had dirty blonde hair and stood tall in front of me. He looked down and said "fuckin' nigger." Then something hit me in the eye. The nasty fool had spit on me!!! And said, "Go back to where you came from!"

I crouched down as he walked away, wiping my eye with my sleeve. When I could see again, I ran home, ran up to my room and started to cry. I felt sick to my stomach. People back home would say 'Nigger' at times, but I never heard it being said with such nastiness and hate. He was white and saying that word. I didn't understand why he would do that. I never did anything to him; I mean did he really not like me because I am black? I did not know who to talk to. I was scared, shocked and knew it was no longer going to be safe for me to walk home from school or anywhere for that matter. I thought of speaking to Mother, but then thought she would just get mad, and besides, she would not do anything about it anyway.

I never saw that kid again, but the damage was done; I was violated and began to believe that white people do not like us black skin folks. Maybe that is why the white skinned lived all by themselves back home in their little corner of our island.

The more days I spent at school, the more certain I became that Mr. Jackson thought I was stupid! When I met him the first time with my mother I knew he was a phony. He had used the kind of condescending tone teachers back home used for a kid with a mental disability. He seemed nice to my mother, yet with me he was mean!

One time, when we were in the middle of class, I was minding my own business, writing in my book, when a couple of kids started whispering behind me. At the time I noticed, but I didn't think anything of it until a booming voice from the front of the room startled me.

"Fatima," said Mr. Jackson, "no talking in class!" I looked up.

"Buuut... but I wasn't talkin"- I stammered.

"Go sit outside if you won't behave," he said sternly, then waited for me to get up, take my things, and head for the door. God, how I wanted to talk back to him! That would just get me in more trouble though, so I bit my tongue.

This continued during several classes and the kids began to notice what Mr. Jackson did. One time, several of them sat around me with their strange little smiles.

"What?" I said.

"We're going to try an experiment," said a little brown boy whose name I've forgotten. "We're all going to whisper during class and see if Mr. Jackson kicks you out again."

Sure enough, Mr. Jackson kept turning his head in my direction every time one of them so much as opened his or her mouth! I kept my head down, obviously focusing on my book, to make sure that he didn't punish me for what they were doing. It didn't work. The kids kept on whispering during class. I think they eventually got bored and frustrated that they never got the credit for their actions. One time some kid said, "It was us, Mr. Jackson!" I was making my way out of the room when I heard that and I turned my head quickly. "We were just doing that to get Fatima in trouble!" I could not believe my ears.

"Doesn't matter who it is," he said. "No one talks. Fatima can serve as an example for the rest of you." My face heated up and if my skin wasn't so dark I would have looked like a bright red apple. I was mad. I knew he hated me and now I hated him.

So, I was convinced Mr. Jackson thought I was stupid. He insisted I sit at the back of the class. I would raise my hand to answer questions and I always knew the answer, but he never picked me. Not only did I not get picked in class, when we had sports teams I would be the last one to be chosen and they would be upset that I was on their team. They considered me to be the bad luck charm.

As he was handing out our report cards before Thanksgiving weekend, Mr. Jackson said, "I'm sorry, Fatima," in a loud voice, "but these grades aren't impressive. You need to get your reading comprehension and math higher."

I took the report card and looked at it. Well below average in English language comprehension. I didn't say it out loud, but all I could think was "just who the hell does he think he is?" followed by "Mother's going to flip out when she sees this." The thought crossed my mind that he was marking me down because he thought I was stupid and I was a black girl from the Caribbean.

That's when it all made sense; the funny-looking smiles, as if he was looking at a misbehaving pet. The slow way he spoke to me and Mother, pronouncing all of his words clearly and slowly. Who did he think he was? He didn't know me and he had no idea that being from the Caribbean meant I spoke the Queen's English.

But there was one surprise in this whole mess. Hours later, I showed that report card to Mother. I remember she was at the kitchen table, eating a bite of rice and beans from her plate, just staring off into space after a long week.

"I got my report card today," I said, trying to hide the quiver in my voice as I approached. Without making eye contact, she took it from me, looked at it, then handed it back. "You can do better next time," she said, then turned back to her meal. That was pretty much her entire attitude towards my schooling. Nothing more I can do now. Just do better next time.

I prayed to make it through the year and never see Mr. Jackson again. At the end of the year, he failed me, so I had to repeat Grade Four. "I don't think Fatima is able to keep up with the other children," he said to Mother, "and it would be better for her to repeat the grade." He later made up some lie that repeating the grade would allow me to be around kids my own age because I had come into Grade Four a year younger than most of the others. It was ridiculous, and besides, everything that he had covered in class, I had already learned in Barbados; however, nothing seemed to matter to this "educated" white man in the big city!

***

On nights when she had to work, Mother would arrange for her boyfriend Glenn to show up and watch me. I didn't like him at all. He had a big belly, and big lips, and half the time, he wouldn't show up at all, leaving me in the house alone. When he was there, Glenn didn't talk much. Sometimes he'd try to help me with my math homework. Even though that was kind of him, overall I didn't care for him. I much preferred my Uncles, who were always willing to act as tutors.

"You should learn to wash the dishes," Glenn said to me one night when I was bringing the dishes back from the dinner table. "Here, let me show you how," he said. Reluctantly, I went over to the sink. "Why do I have to learn this?" I asked him.

"Because if you can reach the sink, you can wash the plates," was his answer.

Glenn! I didn't know what gave him the idea that he could stick his nose into my family's business. He even told me once to stop calling mother "Big Eggie," one of the few terms of endearment we shared as my mother would call my "Little Eggie." I will never forget when she called me that for the first time. At first I had no clue what she was saying and then when I realized she was being nice to me, I officially became "Little Eggie," and that was my first real smile with my Mother since I had been in Toronto.

"No, Fatima," he said, "you must call her either "mom," "mummy" or "mother." Who was this man to tell me what to call my Mother? He wasn't one of my Uncles from Barbados. Still, under his pressure I decided to call her "Mother."

All I knew was that on days when he was with me, I would have to go to bed at 7:30 p.m. I never saw him come or go, but I knew he was there because of the unmade pull out of bed the next morning. When Glenn had skipped out enough times, Mother arranged for me to stay with friends she had in the building until she got home.

After some time, I began to spend weekends with my Godparents. My God mother, Lottie started taking me to Church; an Anglican one in our neighbourhood. She would give me candy to keep me quiet during the service. It was with her that I learned how to say prayers at night before bed.

"Now I lay me down to sleep I pray the Lord my soul to keep, if I should die before I wake I pray the Lord my soul to take."

Up until this point, I hadn't given any thought about what made people alike. In Barbados, majority had black skin like me; there were brown people and light skinned people, but for the most part we were all the same. Everyone more or less shared the same beliefs and values about everything you could imagine in life.

Canada was not that place. From everything I'd heard and seen, this was supposed to be a multicultural melting pot, filled with different religions, skin-tones, beliefs, foods, cultures and attitudes. However, Toronto, at that point, was mostly white English-Canadians. This meant that almost everyone around me was a stranger in this strange land and I trusted no one.

***

As each day passed, I began to lose hope that Ma and my uncles would come to get me. Like a flickering candle getting swallowed up in its own wax, the idea grew dimmer and dimmer. With every joke about my black skin, every laugh at the sound of my accent, every bad mark I got from condescending white teachers and every undeserved insult I got from the kids in the playground, I started to build a box around myself. These tall walls kept out the stresses and the sadness that came my way. My only safe place was by myself, in my room, under my bed sheets as my tears soothed me to sleep. My days of having fun and being a kid were gone. The smell of Ma's cooking and the love inside Baby's hugs were things that I could only dream about; they both abandoned me and this was now my life...

Knock, Knock: Heavenly Father Are You There?

Chapter Three

"God doesn't give you more than you can handle." I remember how often she said that to us. Even though Ma was not religious, she certainly knew every word of the bible. Even though I could not see or hear God, I would say this was one of the first times in my life where remembering those words made me feel like maybe I was going to be okay. I was faced with my first wall at 8 years old. Looking back I can see how that wall on my path defined my anger and embedded it deep inside of me. With each passing comment from the kids at school, the failing marks, and every tear that dropped, a new brick was added, causing that wall to reach higher and higher until all that was in front of me was a solid defence against the world.

Life for me was about surviving each day. As a child, I counted the hours until I got home and then sadly, even counted the hours until I could lay safe in my bed. As I look back now as a Mom, I feel sad for my little self.

By the time I was 10, I was already very independent. I could clean, cook, do my own homework, walk myself to school and even keep myself entertained. Other than my chores, I did not do much. I missed my cousins, I missed my old life and most of all, I missed that little girl who used to play on the beach every Sunday.

Just like that, my life was about to take another turn, but this time I was feeling full with excitement. Mother was pregnant. I laugh as I remember this. I always wondered how was that possible? I mean, I was young, yet I have learned a thing or two about how babies were made and Glenn was always sleeping on the pull out couch. I get now how my mom limited what I saw and heard.

The television show "Roots" had just started to air and it was the talk of my house. It was a big deal and it become very popular. You can imagine what it was like to have a show of all black people. It was nice to see people who looked like me and my family on television. It was February 1977 and my mom's belly was getting large. I had never seen this happen before. I mean Aunty Baby did not have any children and my cousins were dropped off at Ma's house already grown, like me, at the time. I remember watching my mom waddle as she walked and rubbed her belly. We called the baby "Kizzy" or "Kunta Kinte." I was allowed to come up close and touch her as the baby was kicking. One time the baby kicked, it startled me as I could not believe something was alive in there. A big part of me could not wait until she came out, even though I was not sure how she was going to come out, other than knowing God would pull her outta there somehow. When I asked my mom, she just said "never mind, one day you will know and it better not be too soon." After she said that, I perked up and I gave her one of my looks.

Mother's belly became really big and it was time for her to go to the hospital. I spent the week with my Aunt Pam, and on May 3, 1977, my baby sister was born. Excited, I shouted, "Kizzy's arrived!" I was joking, but only about her name. I was so excited! Mother called me over to introduce her to me and said "this is your sister Jane." Oh my God, she was so cute. She had these big fat cheeks, so much hair and she was like the cutest little doll I had ever seen.

Our house quickly became a lot noisier, from the cries during the night, to my mom and Glenn arguing, and the rushing around to get through the day. Mother said it was time to move. We soon moved from a one bedroom, to a two bedroom apartment in the same building. We were lucky because a boy who was in my class was moving out and I right away told Mother. Life was starting to look a little bit better. I had this cute, chubby, kid sister, with lots of hair, and best of all, I finally had my own room!

To my surprise, I found out that Glenn was not moving in with us. I mean he was Jane's daddy and I thought for sure him and Mother were going to get married. This was getting way too complicated for me. He slept over alot and never moved in and to top it all off Jane's last name was his. I did not understand why I had Mother's last name and my half-sister Jane had her Dad's.

I was that kid who always wanted to know why, why, why? Too many why's usually cost me a whooping or two, but I could never control myself. I mean the questions were always right there, nagging me! You know those thoughts that seem to control your mouth? It's just like an out of body experience where you can see and hear yourself saying exactly what is going on in your head and you want to stop it, yet you can't? Well that was me and still is, yet now I have discovered that asking questions improves communication. God created questions for us to ask. When people hear "why" it is like I am speaking a foreign language. What I have learned is that communication will either make or break any relationship.

I remember rushing home from school one day as I needed to get home to take care of Jane. I thought to myself, Ma and Baby would be so proud of me. I was cooking, cleaning the house, changing diapers, feeding the baby, bathing her and even taking her out for walks. I thought maybe if they saw how grown up I was, Ma and Baby would want me back. I was a big girl now; however, what sucked was I was not allowed to go out and play with my friends until all those things were complete. I had finally made friends in the neighborhood, and by the time I did all my chores, everyone had to go home.

Things were changing at home. Mother got a new job working in the rehab department, at a hospital, and was now working Mondays to Fridays during the day, which meant no more shift work or weekends. Since I had lived with her, I had not seen her much as she was always busy. When she was home, she was frantic about what needed to be done. The only time we had together was at the dinner table. For the most part, our conversations consisted of what I did not do and what was needed to get done. With baby Jane here now, our focus was on her, and there really was no time for me to hope that Mother and I would ever talk. .

Over time, I got used to my life in Canada. Barbados still lingered with a subtle ache in my heart, especially whenever we'd get a letter from Ma. I missed my cousins and the sound of the continuous crashing of the waves on the beaches during those Sunday trips, but the lifestyle in Toronto was growing on me. Besides, it's not like I had a choice. This was, as I was repeatedly told, my home. I had some new friends, my day to day routine, I kept out of trouble and I had a new baby sister. Yet one thing's for sure, I would never, ever get used to this cold. I hated winter!

Over the next three years things became much better. As the saying goes, "what doesn't kill you, makes you stronger" and I was certainly not dead. I can now say I evolved into a strong, resilient, independent girl and I could also swing a good punch here and there! I had adjusted and felt like I was becoming a full-fledged "Canadian" kid. Compared to my first traumatic year, it was looking like smooth sailing. What I do know is that this time of my life was an important part of my story. It had a big part in creating the woman I am today. As children we become what we learn. Life is all about learning. We are not born knowing how to be angry, afraid or hateful, it is our life experiences that provide us with these dispositions. It is clear that the year I was left in Canada, with no warning and not one person asking me what I wanted, had me evolve into this bitter woman who refused to trust anyone. As much as hate festered inside me during my childhood, I do recall moments where my heart and mind began to feel something new. I was making friends and settling in. I began to prove to myself that even if I was a misfit, I was still having conversations with God and He was listening.

Knock, knock, "Heavenly Father, are you there?" I was taught by my Godmother to kneel at my bedside to pray and say a traditional bedtime prayer. At times I felt lazy and figured that God wouldn't mind it if I lay in my bed and stared at the ceiling while we had a conversation. Sometimes it seemed to me like I had to knock pretty hard on God's door to get him to hear me, and while there's a chance that sometimes I was only having conversations with my ceiling, it gave me great comfort believing that somewhere up there, someone was listening. God for me, was like an imaginary friend you could talk to without having people call you crazy!

I would often remember the warm days in Barbados when the heat was so heavy and just when I couldn't take it anymore I would say, "oh God, I wish I could be in the ocean to cool my hot skin!" In those moments a heavy breeze would come in from nowhere and surround my body. I would close my eyes, stand still and feel what I imagined the arms of angels wrapping themselves around me would feel like. I would stay in moments like this when I could not prove why things happened. I would look up to the sky, close my eyes and smile.

At a young age, I quickly learned that you do not always have to see something to believe it. When we are blocked by our circumstances it can appear like this brick wall that looks impossible to get over; however, when you are pushed up against it, and there is no other direction you can go, you find the courage, strength and faith to get over it. Getting over the walls in life is what we all deal with and one thing I am certain about is when we hit a wall in life, God provides a ladder.

Mrs. Anita was just that for me - a ladder. She was the one who mentored me to develop myself at school. I believe she saw herself in me and for that reason took the time to help me realize how smart I was. Along with Baby, Conliffe and Mackie, she was one of the few people that made me feel like I was special. What most adults do not realize is that what we say and do to children impacts them. In fact, it is part of the blueprint that moulds them into who they will become as adults. As much as I had bad experiences with teachers, I also had great ones and for that reason I was able to experience the difference and ensure that when I become a mom, I would always play a big role in my children's education.

Mrs. Anita's beautiful smile, smooth voice and patience allowed me to trust her and feel safe that she had my back. All she wanted was the best for me and because of her I excelled in grade 4 and received the "Student of the Year" award!

In grade 5, I fell in love with music when I learned how to play the recorder. I was starting to see that school here in Canada gave you different options and opportunities we did not have in Barbados. My love affair with 'the arts' became a big part of me; you would always catch me singing and humming as I did my chores; I would sing to my baby sister; and the songs in my head would keep me company as I walked to school. My passion for music grew with each day and one day my mother's friend offered to teach me to play the piano. I practiced the piano for 10 years and it was one of the greatest achievements of my life. Music saved me. I heard God in the melodies and it was my private escape.

Living in Canada, there were so many different sports and activities that kids did. I will never forget my first experience skating! I had never seen skates before. I mean, who would make a boot, with a sharp blade on the bottom of it? At least that was my first impression. You can imagine that "ice" much less "ice rinks" are hard to find in Barbados. It was even a luxury to have in hotels back then and having it in your home was unheard of, never mind a gigantic sheet of it. I was told I needed to put them on, stand up, walk over to the ice and skate. No one told me that once I finally got these things on that I needed to be able to balance myself. So, I began with trying to balance. Once I got that down I began to walk thinking: this is great! What they did not tell me is that once I hit the ice, it would be very slippery. You can imagine what happened next. Yup, I landed very quickly on my ass! Thank God I did not get hurt. I looked quickly to see who could have seen me, making sure I was in the clear. I spent the rest of the time just learning how to glide. After several visits to the ice, I eventually became this ordinary Canadian kid who could skate. It was not my favourite thing to do, but I felt like less of a misfit once I'd gotten better at it. Today, every time my feet are cold I go back to this memory as no amount of socks in the world could keep my feet warm when we went skating. I really hate cold feet.

Grade 6 marked the last year of my schooling at Rose Avenue Public School. That year we also moved homes to another area. Mother insisted I continue there so I would not interrupt my schooling. As much as I was angry at my mother, I could see that she cared, as it was not convenient for her to keep me at that school, but believed it was important for my educational progress. Looking back, I can see that she did make sacrifices for me. She also arranged babysitting with my sister's babysitter in the old building so I could go straight there after school until she could pick us up. Eventually it did not work anymore and I had one of my first experiences feeling like a grown up. I remember that moment clearly. I learnt to take the bus, on my own, all the way home.

At times, I would take the bus straight to Mother's job. When I would arrive, she would tell me to go off to the side. I never heard or saw her tell anyone I was her daughter. I had good manners, I was quiet, I did not ask questions and I behaved myself, so I never understood why she gave the impression she did not want anyone knowing she was my mom. I hated this feeling as all it did was remind me, once again, of what it feels like to be unwanted by Ma, Aunty Baby, the kids at school and Mother. Yes! I would say my mind was filled with plenty of evidence where I was unwanted. Just like everything else, I'd get over it. Each time I went there I simply kept my head down, minded my own business and repeated what I heard from almost every adult throughout my young life, "Kids are to be seen, not heard."

Before long, it was June of 1980, and elementary school was over. I remember walking through those hallways one last time like it was yesterday. My memory of that first year of school, of being picked on for my accent, my hair and the color of my skin had stopped , but had turned into being made fun of for my body. I hit puberty earlier than most girls. I was getting taller and most of the boys only reached my boobs. Now, it wouldn't really matter, except for the fact that those boobs were growing and they certainly stood out. As a young woman, and even up until the journey of writing this book, my body image was always dependant on compliments. I would look in the mirror and all I saw was that 11 year old girl, who, because she was skinnier than most, was told repeatedly she had chicken legs. Who could also forget that white kid who spit in my face and called me "nigger." The one thing that impacted me the most and stayed with me well into my early 40's was being told never to smile because I had a big mouth with big teeth. All of that was drilled into my head. I believed I was not pretty and I left this school feeling like an outcast. The same way I had entered was the same way I was leaving. My last walk down that hallway felt like forever! As I walked out the door, my skin felt that first breath of fresh air and I felt nothing but relief.

Oh My God, There He Was!

Chapter Four

There are times in life when you experience pivotal moments that will forever mark your psyche, like the phat cat tattoo I permanently placed on my kitty. When we're born, our life does not come with a manual, nor can you do a Google search on what to expect. Our brain discovers things, and when it experiences a sensation that makes us feel love and aliveness, we want to hold on to that experience and never let go.

Life comes with the good, the bad and the ugly, and I certainly felt like I had, had my fair share of ugly for the last 3 years. I felt free as I left that school, never to return again, with the summer holidays upon me. That summer we moved into our new home. Mother had broken up with Glenn and I did not know why. I do not recall any argument or incident. Like other parts of her life, she kept that from me too. I was surprised, but at the same time it didn't seem that important. All I know is that he helped us move into our new condo and after that I never saw him again.

I spent most of the summer looking after my baby sister, organizing our new home and enjoying the weather. Grade 7 was calling my name: a new school, new friends and a new time in my life. The shock and betrayal of being brought to a new country against my will had also done its part to shape who

I was and who I would become; almost as much as the blessings of spending my early childhood living in the Caribbean culture under the hot Bajan sun.

Somewhere between heartache and blessings is a space filled with so many unknown questions. It can, at times, appear dark, grey and hopeless. Yet, I have learned that we can only relate to these dark spaces as we do when we have reached a new milestone in life; one that is rich with blessings, with love and with hope. With cautious optimism, I was ready to turn a new page in the next chapter of my life with all the beautiful surprises that awaited me.

***

Today is the day. Out with the old and in with the new. Grade 7 is upon me. By this time, I am already quite grown up. I am a survivor, tough and for the most part always alone. Baby Jane cannot engage in conversations with me, so I basically spent most of the time talking to myself. At the time, I basically convinced my brain that, for better or worse, my inevitable fate that I should spend most of my life alone. I mean who needed people anyway? They really were a pain in my ass. They just want you to do chores, tell you not to speak or leave you. Mother's mental manipulations, constant disapproval and the day-to-day shit kicking at school had fortified those walls I built around me. It was safe and secure inside my box of protection, which kept everyone else out. If no one could get in, I would not get attached, or feel the pain and betrayal when they would inevitably leave. Instinctually, whatever child-like innocence I still had, needed protection at all costs. From greeting everyone with a brave face and my sharp tongue, it was clear that no one was gonna fuck with this chick!

I was only 12 when I had already decided what kind of man I wanted, and because of that decision, for the next 25 years, I compared every man I met to this light skinned 13 year old hottie who sat next to me in my classroom. He became my hero. A hero, that came in and vanished like my pair of size 5 Jordache jeans!

It was my first day of school. Grade 7 was finally here. I woke up that morning with a different feeling in my tummy. I mean it was the first day of school and I should typically be feeling gassy, bloated and anxious. That was how most of my days started since I've been in Canada, but this time it was different. My heart was fluttering: a blend of anxiousness and excitement mixed in with a dash of "what the hell am I doing?" I was a big girl now with boobs. I slipped on my new Jordache jeans, brushed my teeth extra hard, put on a little Vaseline and headed to school. I sang as I walked to school because singing always brought me peace. I arrived to find a flood of kids surrounding the front doors. I walked straight through. I noticed I wasn't the only black kid. There were a few more here, so that was good. I kept my head down as I walked through the halls, though I recall seeing another older, black girl walking towards me. As we passed one another I looked straight at her and we both smiled. I could see the comfort and compassion in her eyes.

For the most part, everyone was white. I spoke to God in that moment saying, "please God, make this first day of school easier for me," as I walked into my classroom. There were girls giggling, some kids with their heads down on their desks, the teacher writing something on the board, and… there he was. OH MY GOD, there he was!!! Beyond the fact that I could not believe there was another black kid in my class, he was a boy, and wow, was he cute. All I know is I zoned in on him and then it was like the parting of the red sea as all the bratty girls were sucked in and washed away to the side to make room for me to walk directly over to him.

I stood right there, looked down, he looked up, our eyes locked, and then he just looked back down at his sketch. The guy had this big afro, a black t-shirt, ripped jeans and running shoes. He was doodling something on that paper and looked as miserable as Mothers face when she disapproved of what I was doing. However, I did not care. He was black, and I was not alone, and besides he was cute, so that was a bonus.

The seat next to him was empty and it was going to be all mine.

"Alright, everyone," the teacher said, "please take your seats. I'm going to take attendance. Kevin, Dana, ….okay, Joy, Colin …okay…"

Something caught my eye on top of his head. It was a little white bit of lint, the kind you'd get from your Christmas sweater when it was too dry in the house.

"Got fluff," I said to him, and I reached up and picked it off with my fingers. He glanced at me just as the teacher called my name. "Devonish, Fatima." I raised my hand high in the air. "Present," I said. The teacher smiled and went back to her list. "Gould, Ronald." He raised his hand just above his eyebrow. "Here," he said in a deep voice that seemed to come from his feet, and then went back to his doodling.

"Ronald Gould." Huh, now that was a name! The sound of his voice made my heart beat faster and just like that, it made me feel like life was going to get better.

For the next couple of weeks, Ron barely said a word to me in homeroom. The routine was the same. I'd come in, see him there doodling or writing and sit down next to him. Ron was a mystery. I had a lot of questions. What was up with that same swelled-up face all the time like someone had just peed in his porridge? Where did all of that fluff come from in his hair? Most of all, why didn't he say anything to me?

Ron never took notes in class. He just drew: nothing big, mostly faces, buildings, airplanes, that kind of thing. If this was art class, he'd have been the star pupil. I grew up learning not to ask questions in fear of getting in trouble and resorted to conversations with myself, pretending to answer for the other person. Yet, I wanted to know so much more about this Ron guy and I patiently waited with the hope that he would speak. Regardless, just having him there and watching him everyday was good enough for me.

One day my destiny changed. That fluff was in his hair again. I was, and still am, a clean freak. Mother always had the house spotless, so you can imagine a piece of fluff on a big ass black afro was driving me nuts. So, I picked it out. He normally just shot me an emotionless sideways stare, but this time he turned his head directly towards me. Our faces were looking straight on at one another. His eyes looked right into mine and with a very annoyed expression he said,

"You know," calmly in that rich deep voice of his, "you really need to stop that."

We looked at each other. I was pleasantly surprised. We were stopped and I know I felt a sensation flood my body. I grinned and so did he. Oh yeah, we were going to be great friends!

From that moment, we hung out and became friends. In fact there was a group of us that got close and I felt like I fit in. Life really took a turn for the better. We mainly only hung out at school, not afterwards. Mother was very strict. She would not let me go to other people's homes or go out with my friends. I had chores at home and was responsible for cooking and cleaning, so that had to take priority.

Junior high was really different. My early years, in Canada, consisted of me longing to get to my bed to cry myself to sleep, and now, I could not wait to get home and go to bed so I could wake up and go to school the next day. Now that's a big change! When I would walk to school I'd always be able to find Ron by the Junction. It was a spot past a row of houses near Broad Acres School where these big, brilliant, pink roses would grow in the warmer weather. Every time I saw a pink rose I would think of Ron. Each morning coming up to the Junction he would be there being all cool, waiting for me.

Ron's favorite word was "cool." He would say it in such a calm way that it actually sounded unique. He did not speak much, yet when he did, it was always straight, simple, and for the most part, he was nice. His general response to everything was "cool." Whenever he would say that four letter word to me, I would grin from ear to ear. Before long, I made other friends and there was a group of us that hung out together. Elizabeth, Sam, Robert, Ron and myself. I always had to go straight home after school and that walk home was basically the only social life I had. Unless my mom knew the parents of my friends, I was not to go over. She believed in avoiding getting into trouble, so it was best not to go over to anyone's house, especially if there were men there. Mother always told me she could not protect me if she's not around. I never asked why. I just did what I was told.

Mother worked late, so if I was not allowed to go over to their houses, the best solution was for them all to come to mine. Of course, Mother did not know this, but a girl needs to do what a girl needs to do! For months we would meet at my house after school. My friends would hang in the den and play records, 8 tracks or sometimes just listen to the radio-loudly. We would sing, dance and laugh. While they were here I would also need to go cook and clean, but it did not matter as I felt as though I was part of something special. This was the greatest thing that happened to me since I was left here in Canada. It did not matter that they were having fun without me at times. My new friends liked me for me. They never picked on me or made me feel left out. For the first time in my life, I belonged. I was lean, pretty well developed and saw myself as not bad looking. The boys would watch me run around in gym class, stare at me and smile. I would look at them thinking what is wrong with these "fools?" I later figured out it was because they thought I was cute! Now that was a turn in a different direction. Look at me, Miss Fatima Devonish, a "hottie"!

Our group of friends became close. What is interesting is after all those butterflies in my tummy with Ron, at the start, it turned into a close friendship instead. Besides, I had made it clear to everyone that there was no way I would ever be able to have a boyfriend. We knew the rules and I loved our group.

It was February of 1980 and we were all hanging out at my house as usual. The music was playing and we were grooving to our favorite tunes. Elizabeth and Sam were going out by that time. There was a new girl at school named Morgan and her and Ron hooked up. Robert and I were the single ones in the bunch and I was not interested in him as more than a friend. Besides he was white! I wasn't into white boys and I sure as hell knew they were not into me.

For most of my life I believed you just don't mix black and white as there were so many stories about that back home. I guess for me, when I thought of white boys, all I could recall was the one who spit in my eye and called me a nigger. As I grew up, I could see as an adult that I had inherited the views of my ancestors, specifically around skin color. Not only did I personally experience the wrath of discrimination, I was also not an angel. See, I judged those white girls and I certainly judged white boys. Today, I am grateful to God that that belief system has left me. Now, when I see others, I see them as persons and not a color.

Every once in awhile it still creeps up in my thoughts. In fact, just recently I was in a shoe store trying on some shoes. They were high, hot and sexy. This man who was watching me said, "those look great on you." I took a double take and quickly went inside my head and said, "he's white- that white man just gave me a compliment." I said, "thank you" and tried on a different pair. He then said, "No, I like the other ones better, you have great legs." I smiled and said "thank you" again. In that moment I realized that he was just a 'man who was attracted to me and it didn't matter that he was white'

So here I am, in the kitchen, making dinner, while the R&B music carries throughout the condo. I do not know what Robert had been doing, but he was the first one to hear the latch turning on the front door. He rushes over to me stricken with panic and fear. "Your Mother is home early!" My heart sinks! I freeze! In that moment, I feel suffocated like I cannot breath. Elizabeth and Sam are in my bedroom with the curtains closed and making out. The rest are in the Den. Mother walks in. She stops. The condo was small, but I had this foolish hope she could not see them. Who was I fooling? There it was: "the look." The look of death. Her eyes met mine staring deep into my consciousness reminding of who I was and who I was not. I did something wrong, in her home, and I realized I am not good enough. Once again, I disappointed her.

Could God hear me? Was it fair for me to ask Him to save me when I was so obviously guilty? My Mother stayed in the kitchen. I quickly head for the den and closed the kitchen door behind me to go see and make sure everyone was all there. Their faces were shocked, flushed and unsure of what to do next. We were caught and I knew I was the one that was going to take the fall.

"We can't let Fatima get in trouble for this!" said Elizabeth.

"But what can we do?" asked Sam.

That's when Ron said, "Follow me, guys." We lined up at the kitchen door with Ron at the front and me at the very back. We were lined up like little grade 8 teenage soldiers.

He opened the swinging doors. Mother was sitting on her seat in the kitchen. She looked up. Her face still the same from the last look she gave me. That's when Ron did something I did not expect. While everyone else loitered around looking scared and ashamed, Ron stepped forward with his head held high and his shoulders back.

"Mrs Devonish," he said with a firm, calm voice.

Mother's eyes widened while the rest of her face was stoic. Silently listening, you could see she was a little taken aback and waiting to hear what this young man was about to say.

"It's not Fatima's fault. It's ours. We wanted to all hang out and we bugged Fatima to have it here. Please, don't punish her for what we've done."

The air in my lungs left me! You could see the heads of the others look at Ron, then look at Mother, and then back at Ron like a slow motion tennis match. I was in awe.

Mother looked Ronald up and down, saying nothing for a moment while she considered what he'd said. I thought they were all going to take my licks.

That pause seemed so long.

Ron broke the silence and spoke again.

"Ms. Devonish it is not all Fatima's fault and she should not get blamed. What can we do?"

Mother's faced shifted, she looked surprised, with that heaviness all over her face. With a stern clear voice she said:

"Son, go home. I think you should get yourself home young man.

And that was it. Ron looked over to all of us and back to Mother; he smiled politely; gave this nod with his head to direct everyone out. They got their coats and they all left.

I stood in the kitchen and my feet felt nailed to the floor. There was a heavy silence. I stared hard at the wall to avoid making eye contact with her. The crack of her voice started. Her tongue lashed out at me. As she threw out the insults and the names, part of my brain shut off and she sounded muffled. I drifted into my thoughts. I was thunderstruck. Ron had done the impossible. He had stood up to my mother.

Not only did he stand up to her, he stood up for me. No one had ever stood up for me before. This was something new. I never experienced this feeling before. I did not know what it was. It felt like something unfolding from my core; a joyful caress of bliss all over my body with a flutter inside my chest and tingling between my legs. I should have been terrified of the wrath of Mother's next actions, but I was consumed with thoughts of wonder.

I was quickly snapped out of it by Mother's stern voice as she raised her voice. "Go to your room. NOW!" And I did. The walk to my bedroom was filled with shame for getting caught. Regardless of how mean Mother was, at times, I was the one who had lied. I did something I knew I shouldn't have done and this time she actually had the right to be mad at me.

I lay awake in my bed, staring at the ceiling. I started talking to God, which quickly shifted into replaying what went down in my head over and over again. Seeing Ron, standing there, looking directly at Mother. I don't get it. He barely speaks and here he was standing up for me and speaking to my mom, not wanting me to take all the blame. Who was this guy? In the quiet privacy of my own bed, I stepped out of my safe zone and allowed my imagination to wander beyond the walls and barricades I'd erected against the world, in awe of the boy who had surprised me so completely. Ronald Gould, this light skinned black knight, with his big ass afro and ripped jeans. Lord have mercy. My soul was marked and Ron had marked it.

NEVER AS GOOD AS THE FIRST TIME

Chapter Five

Good times come and go, some last longer than others and then there are those special moments that will forever mark you. I am referring to the life altering times of "firsts," when destiny serves you on a platter, the thrill of a rush. A moment in time that you never regret and wish lasted forever. Memories that are so real, so vivid it's like they happened yesterday. The magical gifts of life fulfill and satisfy every part of who we are.

My last thought before I went to sleep was seeing Ron stand up to Mother. He looked like a statue of hope. It was my first taste of what it looked like on the flip side of being alone. The side where you trust people, get close to them and know they have your back. These feelings were so foreign to me, and still I wanted to hold on tight and never let go. The morning arrived and my eyes were opened bright. My first thought was of Ron however quickly switched over to me saying out loud, "oh dear, I have to face Mother."

I got ready for school. When I went to the kitchen, there she was. She did not look at me or say good morning. I could not really eat my breakfast as my belly was all messed up. I put on my jacket, grabbed my books and said bye as I approached the door. My mother's way of dealing with things when she was really angry was to say nothing at all and accompany that with a look that could kill. That is when I know I've crossed the line. At that moment I wish she would just ground me like ordinary Canadian parents. The silence and awkwardness made me sick to my stomach.

It bothered me for the first 5 minutes or so walking to school and then my mind filled with thoughts of Ron. I arrived at school and met up with the gang. They huddled in tightly all wanting to know what happened after they left. I just told them that my mother hadn't spoken one word to me since and I hid out in my room all night. The truth is, my life didn't change that much. Every day I'd get up, go to school, do my chores and then go straight to my room anyway. Mother didn't speak a word to me for a week. I went from bliss to busted. I didn't see Sam or Elizabeth and Ron wasn't even at the Junction on the way to school. Everyone was giving me space until the heat was off. I knew they all were feeling really bad and seeing me just made them feel guilty.

One day when I came home from school, Mother was already home. She was on the phone. She decided to call up all of her brothers and sisters. "Do you know what Fatima did?" she said loudly in her full Bajan accent. "She had all these people over at my house messing up the place. And boys, too!"

So here I am, walking into a shit storm of total humiliation with a line up of all my aunts and uncles on the other end of the phone who now think I am prancing around with boys. My mouth drops, frozen, unclear what to say. I could not believe this was happening to me. And just like that, the sex talks began. I am sure if they were in front of me, they would be placing a cross in front of me, waving it back and forth like I was a nasty little whore. Okay, maybe that was a bit dramatic, but who the hell knows. All I know is that I was being stripped of all my privacy and I was totally embarrassed.

I took one last look at my mother and went straight to my room. I could not control how Mother was speaking about me, so I decided to block it out and pulled out my books to study. I was five minutes into reading when I was startled by the sound of Mother's voice as she yelled:

"Fatima, pick up the phone!"

All my friends knew I was laying low until everything was back to normal so I wondered who was calling me.

I came out of my room and walk over to Mother who was still holding the phone. Normally when someone called for me, she just kept it on the counter for me to pick up. But this time, she was holding it out, her face so stern and standing strong like a cadet. I knew she could see that my face went out of sorts by the expression on her face. I took the phone from her.

"Hello?"

"Fatima, this is Vere, your uncle."

I was dumbfounded. His first words to me were, "Fatima do you know what VD is?"

There was a short pause. I was confused and responded with "Um… your name, Vere Devonish?" As that was his name.

"No, venereal disease! It's what you get when you have boys in your room."

My head was swelling with confusion! Dear Lord, what the heck was he talking about? I was not having sex with anyone. Once he was done giving me a lecture and telling me how boys are going to give me diseases, I got off the phone and rushed to my bedroom.

For days, I received call after call from all my aunts and uncles. I spent hours on the phone having the same conversation 7 different ways. One thing was clear, my aunts and uncles seemed like they did not like sex. With each call, Mother seemed to get calmer, like it was working and I would stay away from sex 'till I'm 50.

With the awkwardness, at home, dying down I didn't have to rush home anymore. So I took my time walking home from school. I turned the corner at the Junction and there he was. Standing there, looking straight at me. He gave me that grin and walked me the rest of the way home. In that moment, VD and all that other stuff they were talking about was the furthest thing from my mind. I am certain my Mother would have been very disappointed at the thoughts that were running through my head.

From the moment Ron stood up for me, and throughout our time apart, to walking side by side home after school again, I realized I missed him. And I know I missed him because it was a familiar feeling similar to how I felt about Baby and Ma, Roy and Toni, or how I felt about the warm Bajan sun. Being with Ron that afternoon, allowed me to breathe again and I felt safe. He was now someone I knew I could trust. Just like that, my mind said the words "I love this guy."

There was a sadness about Ron as he was always guarded and secretive. I was never able to figure out what was really going on in his life, but my heart went out to him. I would later learn that he was an adopted child. His mother had given him up, more or less at birth and he lived in foster homes for a couple of years before being adopted by a white family. That was all he shared. He was always the one person that I had a lot of patience with and compassion for.

That night as I was laying down, I got stuck in my head. My thoughts were racing fast and furious. There was so much about Ron that made me want to bring him closer, but at the same time I had so many reasons why we needed to stay just friends. What if we messed it up? I don't want to lose him as a friend. Maybe he doesn't feel the same way about me? He was so damned hard to read. I didn't want to look like a fool. Maybe it's just hormones? What if I get VD? I grabbed my head and yelled "Stop!" I was tired and confused. I just didn't want look foolish, but I knew I wanted Ron. My belly started to ache. When I get stressed my insides twist and turn and just like that, I become a prisoner of my fears.

Winter passed into spring, and warmer weather was finally here! The apple trees beside Broadacres Park were budding and all that stuff about Ron, and hormones, and VD was stored deep inside me. No one needed to know, especially Ron, and just like that, I buried my feelings over and resumed control.

It was May and time for the school dance. There I was, doing my 'prep.' I took so much extra time getting myself ready. This was a special occasion and it required extra care. I had never been to a school dance before. I had only seen them in the movies or on television. I walked in. The gym was pretty empty, which is probably because I was in such a rush to get there that I arrived a bit early.

I saw my friends and walked over. Sam, Elizabeth and Robert were all there.

"Damn! Look how everyone's cleaned up!" I said.

"There is barely anyone here," said Sam.

Elizabeth was to the right of me and said, "No one is dancing."

"Because the boys won't ask, I said.

Robert was standing behind us and sarcastically said, "Don't be stupid, who asks girls to dance anymore? That's just too weird."

Elizabeth stared him down with one of her looks and said, "Is it to weird or are you just too scared?"

Robert stood with his arms tightly crossed saying nothing. Yup! It was clear, he was scared.

"Come on," said Sam "let's go." He took Elizabeth's hand and pulled her towards the dance floor.

I stood there in awe. I had never been to a school dance and I was recalling what I had seen in the movies. There was some of the same stuff: a table with a bowl full of punch and snacks, a couple of overdressed teachers and clusters of kids, a few I saw from my homeroom. Sam was right, there weren't a lot of people there. Not even fifty kids. Elizabeth and Sam came back and we leaned up against the wall.

"I'll go get us some drinks," Elizabeth said, heading over to the table.

I looked over in the direction of where they were serving drinks and about five feet from the corner was Ron chatting with some of his buddies. He saw me, barely a trace of a grin on his face, and tilted his chin back as if to say 'what's up' before going back to his conversation. My cheeks became instantly warm.

"I'm gonna ask him to dance," I said out loud to myself. And right on cue, they started to play the Beatles… "Hey Jude…"

I looked around. Sam and Elizabeth were dancing. Even Robert was on the dance floor, with some Asian girl who's name I never found out. All my friends were dancing except me; ...and Ron. I drummed up the courage and walked over to him. The spinning pink and blue lights were passing across his face. I instantly noticed the little fluffs stuck in his afro. I reached up, picked them out and said, "got fluff."

Ron looked down at me and with a cute sound in his voice said, "Yeah, didn't I say you had to stop doing that?"

I gave him a cheeky grin and said, "and how are you going to stop me?"

Without another word, Ron took my hand in his firm, gentle grip and lead me onto the dance floor. Together, in each others arms, we danced under the colourful lights, letting Paul McCartney's "Hey Jude"... melt my heart.

The lyrics "Remember, to let her into your heart, and you can start, to make it better..." felt like this song was made for us.

There I was, in this life altering moment. My body pressed against Ron's, wrapped in his arms, basking in the essence of my first slow dance. My heart and head were at war. Battling between my feelings of fear and the magic of fate.

"Stop Fatima!" I said loudly in my head. You love this boy. "No, it's impossible, you love the idea of him, it's just your hormones." No! I feel good when I'm near him. "Watch it, or you're going to get hurt; you're just good friends." No, we're more than that. I paused. My last thought was "he does not feel the same way so forget it," and just like that, the song was over.

I realized I wasted our song battling with my own head. Ron released me and I looked into his dark brown eyes. For the briefest moment, I swore I saw something – a glint of feeling, familiar and still somehow new – and I wanted to say something to him, but as quickly as it came, it passed. Ron smiled and we left the dance floor. The moment was gone, and I might have missed my chance, but I danced with Ronald Gould and it was magical! That's when I knew Ron would forever be a part of my life.

After the dance, it kept getting warmer as the end of the school year crept closer and closer. Junior high, oh, what a time this had been. I really experienced big girl things, but I was also going to miss being a kid. My days of childhood were numbered and high school was on its way. High school was going to be all about learning to drive and getting my first job; planning for university and getting into a serious relationship.

One day during recess I was outside reading, when Morgan Dunbar came up to me. She was a new kid that year, and though she wasn't part of our clique, she was someone I'd call an "associate member;" basically a groupie.

"Hey Fatima," she said, approaching the steps out back of the school where I was sitting.

"Hey Morgan," I said, "what's up?"

"Nothing."

She started to slowly twirl the back of her hair in that cute ditzy girl kind of way.

"Listen..." she said with a long silent pause.

I waited for a few seconds, and when she didn't say anything, I said "Yeah?"

Morgan let go of her hair, took a breath, then looked me straight in the eye and asked, "So, are you and Ron a thing?"

I frowned, as I thought to myself that it was a strange thing to ask.

"No," I replied. Morgan smiled and I saw her shoulders relax. I hadn't even realized they were tense.

"Okay! Good, I just wanted to make sure."

Morgan was silent for a moment and still looking at me, so I nodded politely and waited for more. Finally I asked impatiently, "Because....?"

"Ahhh, well... see, I really like him, and I was thinking of asking him out."

What a weird girl, I thought. Sweet, but weird.

"No, you go ahead and do that. We're just friends."

Morgan smiled. "That's great, thanks so much!" She started to walk away and I found myself getting up.

"Hey!" I called. Morgan turned around. "Um… let me know how it goes?"

Morgan grinned. "Sure!" and continued on her way.

As I sat back down, and watched her skip away down the sidewalk, I felt my stomach start to heat up. Mother must have put a little too much hot sauce on my cold cut sandwich and now it was giving me heartburn. I dismissed it and made a mental note to have a glass of water.

Throughout the rest of that warm, sunny day, the feeling didn't go away, and my brain kept coming back to that conversation. Later that night, I was sitting at the dinner table with my sister, my plate of stewed chicken and rice steaming in front of me.

"Fatima," said Mother from the other side of the table, "you haven't touched your food."

"Sorry," I said, picking up my fork. I dug into the rice, but didn't bring anything back to my mouth.

"You need to eat," said Mother. "I didn't just waste two hours making you good food."

"Sorry," I said again, putting the fork down. "I don't feel so good."

"Did the sandwich I made you bother your belly?"

"No, not diarrhea. It's just… I just don't feel good."

Without another word, Mother got up and checked my forehead. "You don't feel sick," she said, and sighed. Getting back up to go to her chair she said, "Just eat what you can and put the rest in a container. Don't waste the food. I work hard for it. You know I work 14 out of every 15 days? That's one day off! I do this to put food on the table, and a roof over your head." Shit! Why was she always this cranky? Always yelling for no reason? It seemed like she was always mad at me, like I went out of my way to do things to piss her off. Going on and on about how all I want to eat is KFC or Mcdonalds. "You think money grows on trees?" God only knows what goes on in her head. What upsets me even more, is she won't say a single harsh word to the love child; in her eyes my little sister can do no wrong.

"KFC isn't bad," I said, staring at my plate. Oh, I shouldn't have said that.

With a loud, firm voice she said, "You know- hey, look at me." I made eye contact with her as she spoke - "You know how I feel about wasting my money making other people rich!"

I nodded and Mother went back to her meal. I sighed and put my hand on my stomach. It wasn't upset. I was hungry but I just didn't feel like eating.

Hours later, when I was laying in bed, I figured out the obvious: why Morgan's question caught me off guard and why I had butterflies. It was because I had a crush on Ronald Gould. So much for 'just friends.'

***

Every time I saw Morgan, her question would swirl around playing games with my head. Quite a bit of time had passed since the last time I was in big trouble for having the gang over and I really wanted my social time. So I figured I'd risk having people over, but no more than two at a time, so if my mother came home early it wouldn't look like a party. We'd listen to WBLK and hang out.

Ron would join us every once in awhile and I wanted to ask him about Morgan, but he never mentioned her. We spent a lot of time talking on the phone. I can't really remember what we talked about, but we always had a lot to say, so despite being separated by distance and only speaking on the phone,

I felt myself growing closer to him.

One day as I was walking home from school, I passed by the Junction, and from the corner of my eye I saw something move. There were two kids my age making out. I looked closer and there she was, Morgan Dunbar, AND the boy was NOT Ron! I remember a massive rush of relief, excitement and weakness with this news and I began grinning like a fool. That was it. This was a sign. I looked up to God and closed my eyes and in that moment took ownership of the feelings I had for Ron.

One day after school, Ron came over, but this time it was just him. I remember he was wearing ripped black jeans, army boots and a plain black t-shirt hidden inside a pale blue denim jacket. I remember the cool, woodsy fall air billowing into the house as he walked in. We shared the couch and listened to the radio together. I was fighting the impulse to take his hand, an instinct that was starting to seem as natural as breathing. However, that was not allowed between two friends. Then, when it was time to go home, Ron and I stood in the hallway, and I decided to let him in on my little secret.

"You know, the other day, I saw Morgan making out with someone near the junction?"

Ron's eyes perked up. "Really?"

Neither of us said anything for a brief moment. Deep inside, I could feel a fluttering nervousness start to build up.

"Did you know that Morgan asked me about you?"

"No," he replied, "when? About what?"

"She wanted to know if you and I were going out."

He laughed. "That's hilarious! What did you tell her?"

The butterflies were starting up again, this time rising into my chest. "Well... I told her it was alright, that we're just friends."

We were standing there, in the hallway, with only a foot between us, in silence.

Finally he said, "She's going to have a hickey."

I grinned, blushing a little. At school every kid with a hickey was prancing around the schoolyard at recess showing off their romantic trophies. It was like an epidemic. The school acted accordingly by sending every student home with a letter to his or her parent/guardian explaining the situation and the possibly dire consequences for their precious offspring if things continued on their present trajectory.

"I think she's going to have more than one," I replied. We laughed, and for some reason, my heart was now pounding in my chest.

I know Ron sensed something was up "Well," he said yawning, "I'd better get home."

I nodded and went over to give him a hug. My senses were suddenly heightened. We were standing in the doorway, with the living room behind us on the left, and the kitchen to the right. Our feet straddled that space in between the two rooms.

I was very aware of the firmness of his chest against mine, the strength of his arms wrapped around me, the smell of soap, his scent and the way his cheek brushed against mine… then I started to let go.

But he didn't, instead he drew me in closer and my lips melted into his. Our first kiss. I was lost in the moment. I felt a warm rush go through my entire body. My heart was pumping against the inside of my chest. Wow! I never wanted it to end. Ron released me and let out a big satisfied sigh and then I kissed him on the neck and gave him a hickey. Wow! That was amazing and I vowed never to forget it. For the rest of my life I measured every kiss against this one.

The Letter

Chapter 6

Everyone loves a good fairytale. I didn't have much exposure to stories like Cinderella and Snow White. I did not play with Barbies and there wasn't any time to be watching cartoons on Saturday mornings. Up until the age of 8 I was working on a farm. Since I'd been in Canada, I was a lot more like Cinderella than I'd care to admit: tucked away in the dark parts of the house, cooking, cleaning and surviving.

I would love to say that after that kiss with Ron, we were an item, but I'd be lying. There was no 'happily ever after' and even though he will always be that Hero in my life, we were only kids, and too young to be in that kind of a relationship. Things never got awkward though. We had a bond and a mutual understanding. We did not need to talk about it either, we always knew it was there. It was our special moment, one we would remember forever.

Junior high was one of the greatest and happiest times of my life. It was short but filled with wonderful memories. The summer passed and high school began. High school was a blend of hard work, new friends, new responsibilities and raging hormones.

Through high school, the gang and I did not stay together like we were before. As the years in high school passed, our friendships drifted. We were all growing up and it wasn't that easy for me to have any kind of life outside of home and school. My friends were all doing the things that typical teenagers do and I was at home being the maid.

Sadly, the majority of my teenage years were spent dealing with the regrets and frustrations of my mother's life, the decisions she made and the wrath of her tongue. Nothing haunts you more than the things you cannot say, like being told not to speak or to not having anyone in your life that makes you feel like you matter. I can count, on one hand, the times in my life where I felt someone had my back. One thing was for sure, I never felt like my mother did. Going through life suppressing how you feel, pretending to be happy and acting like you are strong, when deep inside you are ready to fall apart, is how I trained myself to be so that I could survive. I had been surviving all through my life. When something good happens my brain is convinced, it will not last long. If I love someone, I believe that person will leave me. Life was safe behind my walls. It was easier being alone than having to face the disappointment of becoming a victim.

My relationship with my mother felt like a prison to me. I was old enough to have my own point of view, but not old enough to speak. I had no power and there was nothing I could see to do about it. Mother would always say, "I am the mother, you're the child. You will listen to me, and that's that."

Since we moved to our new condo, Mother would work fourteen days in a row with one day off. The rules of the house were: Fatima makes dinner, cleans the house, does the laundry and looks after little sister, when mother wasn't home, which was pretty much always.

Some days, I felt like much of my childhood was taken away being a housemaid. For the most part, I made it work, but it meant not really doing much else. In high school, I joined the girls' basketball team. We had after school practice and that got me into trouble because I couldn't get home in time to make dinner.

"Why the hell aren't you home to make food? Do you know how hard I work?" If Mother had to pick me up after a late night practice, I would get in the car and her face would go all crooked She would ask rhetorically, "Why you smelling up my car? Disgusting!"

I really liked playing basketball even if I sucked at it, and I would have kept playing if not for the aggravation of constantly listening to her complain about it. So I dropped out. Afterwards, I never joined any more clubs, sports teams or committees. My only source of fun, outside of my friends coming over every so often and visiting relatives, was piano class on weekends. Sleepovers with my friends weren't allowed either regardless if it was at their homes or mine. I was under house-arrest!

Mother's temper grew sharper. Sometimes, something as trivial as a dish in the sink would set her off. She'd yell and threaten to throw things at me. I can only assume it was the stress of being a single mom with two kids and working all the time. On my watch, my sister was well taken care of, and nothing happened to her, but it wasn't enough to ease the worries of my mother. I was never the typical teenager. I lived life doing what I was told, all because of a belief that was deeply embedded in both Mother and myself that children should be seen and not heard.

One day things came to a head. I was in the kitchen when Mother said something in her typically nasty way. I cannot remember her exact words, but it was something about how she can't take this shit. Just like that, I exploded.

I glared at her. I was so angry. I'd had enough of this shit. Years and years of saying 'yes please' caught up with me. I spoke back to her: "I did NOT do anything to cause your sorrows! You should not be taking them out on me!" Mother turned to me with rage in her eyes and reached for the nearest thing she could grab. I moved to the side and ducked, just in case she decided to throw it. She didn't, but I could tell she wanted to.

"You ungrateful manipulative bitch!" Mother shouted. "You have a lip on you. I'll fix you good!"

I headed to my room and slammed the door behind me. When I was sure she wasn't listening, I let myself cry. I sobbed into my pillow, lightening the load my heart had been carrying around all of this time. Then, it was over. I felt relieved and numb. I went to the mirror and wiped my eyes. Staring back at me was this scared, sad little girl who had no power over her own life. How I hated the face looking back at me!

"No one's gonna respect you if you cry," I said to my reflection. "Don't let the wretch see you weak."

Mother and I didn't speak to each other, at all, for the rest of that week, maybe longer.

It should be well-established by now that my mother was a formidable West Indian mom. It was everywhere in her parenting style. Mother's frustration with something I did wrong on any given day could be measured in the distance covered by whatever wooden spoon or spatula she would throw at me from the kitchen. My relationship with Mother consisted of following orders, being the maid and taking her abuse.

I longed to have a relationship with Mother like I heard other kids had. Why was my mine so different? Why did she hate me so much? With every word from her mouth, and everything she threw at me, I resented her more.

***

As an adult every time a woman was nasty and miserable the girls would automatically say, "she must not be getting any!" Women often blame another woman's unhappiness on the assumption that her love life sucks. I wished Mother would meet a man and maybe that would make her happy.

At a New Year's Eve party Mother met Clyde. They started dating and things moved very quickly from there.

By June, he was moving in. By November, they had gotten married. The funny thing about the wedding was that there were four of us who missed the ceremony and I was one of them. My Uncle Vere was supposed to come home to pick us up while Mother and Clyde were at the church, but by the time he got there, the wedding was over. Mother said nothing and I often wondered over the years if it bothered her, at all, that we had missed it.

My grandmother travelled on a plane for the first time in 72 years to come to the wedding. Fortunately she did attend. At the age of 75 my grandmother migrated to Canada to live here for good and is still alive at 101 years of age as this book was written!

So here I am, now I have a stepfather! It all happened so fast and of course no one asked me how I felt about it. I was this girl who cooked, cleaned, got bossed around, yelled at and at times, threatened to have pot covers thrown at her head. I felt I did not belong in my own home and now a man I had little to no relationship with, was living in our house. One more person I was there to serve.

This was my day-to-day living. Whenever there was a plan, I was not included. Mother and Clyde just told me what to do. I kept a journal in those days and I wrote entry after entry about how much I disliked having him around. Clyde was like a king, like the pope: they worshipped the ground he walked on. He was an academic, eloquent and commanding, and expecting only the best at all times from the people in his life. What's more, Clyde rarely spoke to me, even though I had to clean up after him before mother got home.

Mother was taken with him. God, how she was taken with him! She did not allow my sister and I to be ourselves at all in his presence. "Mind what you girls say," she'd tell us, "you don't want to make us sound like idiots in front of this educated man. Don't embarrass me!" Now on top of us being stupid, burdensome or weak, we were also an embarrassment. It hurt of course, how could it not, but I never once gave Mother the satisfaction of seeing my hurt.

Mother worshipped him and he degraded her. I hated Mother for the most part, but I felt sorry for how Clyde treated her. He continuously insulted her, always questioning her knowledge. He wanted to know what she was watching, reading and doing. One day a friend came over to study and witnessed his behaviour and asked me why my mother put up with it when she's accomplished so much as a single mother.

Clyde had a son, his name was Ben and he lived with us for the first year. Just as I seldom spoke with Clyde, I rarely spoke with the son, who was younger than I was. It was like sharing a house with strangers. The extent of our communication was "hi" and "bye." After a year, he moved away permanently to live with his mother in Washington DC.

I had made two new friends in high school: Sophie and Carlin. Thank God for them because they kept me sane. Whenever I told them I was over it and that I was running away Carlin would say: "No. Stay home. It's not the happiest, but it's better than being homeless. Besides, your mother cares about you, this is just her way of showing it, and it's the only way that she knows." Sophie called me every morning to make sure I was up and getting ready for school. She replaced Ron as my walking partner.

As much as I appreciated Carlin for what he was saying about my mother, I could not help but go back and think, how he could be so blind. From there, my mind would drift, recalling the time Ron stood up to Mother. Carlin was sticking up for Mother, and Ron had stood up for me.

***

Before long, high school ended and I was starting college. It was a new time of my life and it gave me somewhat of a break from all the stress and drama. I wasn't really focusing on any particular career, just something that would help me get a good job, benefits and allow me to move out of my mother's house and live a nice, quiet, no-noise-in-my-head life!

I commuted 4 hours a day to get to college. I would leave at 6 am. and return home at 10 pm. I also worked at Bi-Way; a discount clothing store, to pay for my transportation. As exhausting as it was, it felt good to be up to something in the world and be engaged with my own life instead of being a servant to Clyde and Mother.

I may have been spending less hours at home, but I couldn't escape the pain of Mother's injustice. The brutality of her tongue and the spite in her eyes that were pushing me deeper and deeper into a psychological grave where I was burying myself alive. I didn't ask her for much, as I learned to just not bother. She put a roof over my head and fed me. I was clear that was the extent of her commitment towards me. I did not have any expectations of her helping me through school or anything else for that matter. The college offered grants to financially support students and it turned out that I qualified! All I needed was a guardian's signature. The grant would help me work less hours so that I could spend more time on my studies. All I needed was a signature and I was on my way.

I came home. Mother was in the kitchen making rice and peas. Clyde was sitting in the living room watching TV.

"Mother," I started, being very polite and calm, "Could you sign this application form for me?"

Mother didn't look up from her stove. "Can't you fill it out yourself?"

"It requires signatures from my legal guardians," I said, clearing my throat. Clyde looked up from his chair. Mother put her spoon down and looked up. "It's for a grant from the college. It'll help me pay for my tuition and a few bills so I won't have to work as many hours." I glanced over at Clyde. "Will you sign it for me?"

I followed Mother's gaze over to Clyde. He shook his head no and turned back to the TV. She looked back at me. "No, we will not," she replied. Instantly, I clenched my jaw as a burst of raw anger shot up from the pit of my stomach, though I did my best to hide my expression.

"Why not?" I asked in a neutral voice.

"Fatima, if I had to work hard for everything I have, so should you. Clyde worked hard to get where he is. Hard work is what life's about. If that means you have to work more hours at Bi-Way, then you work more hours at Bi-Way."

Mother went back to her cooking, like nothing happened, and I lingered for a few quick seconds before storming off to my room. In the end, though, she was right. I had to deal with the cold, hard reality. I had to survive and that meant working. But I never forgot how a single look from my stepfather, a man not even of my own blood, was enough to convince the woman who had birthed me to sell out on her daughter!

Later, Mother said to me that it would make Clyde look bad if he had signed the paper as it would make people think he was unable to put me through school. What the hell! He wasn't! She just made me angrier. I resented them both even more. "Fuck you!" I said in my head.

Perhaps my mother had a guilty moment because shortly after that she gave me a bus pass. All that did was fuel the rage that was brewing inside my spirit.

The moment my insides felt like they were filling with rage, I called out to God. "Heavenly Father. Please have mercy on me, help me I don't know how much longer I can take this."

After the first year of college, I got a call from my aunt's husband. "Fatima, it makes no sense that you are taking the bus up and down the city to go to school. Why don't you come live by us in Scarborough? You'll save travel time and have more time to relax."

"That sounds nice," I said. "You will have to clear it with my mother." Dear Lord. Thank you, thank you! You really are listening!

Mother said YES! Not that I needed her permission anyways, nor do I think she really cared.

I offered to pay $100 in rent every month. I was also told that, as part of the agreement, I would be home at night while my uncle was out of town working for a railway company. My aunt, meanwhile, was going to take a night shift job at a hospital as a nurse.

Here I am, excited to be living far away from Clyde and Mother, only to find out my Mother already new about the plans in the first place, so of course she agreed. God, people are sneaky. Just like when I was 8. Everyone lied to me. I was only coming for the summer when the truth was I was never returning. I was once again the last to know. The truth is I was working, paying rent, AND I ended up being their full time babysitter. How fuckin' convenient for them!

***

Just like that, life surprised me again! My father had relocated to the Toronto area and he reached out to me.

I spent a lot of time getting to know him and his family. When they met me, they thought I was his daughter from his ex-wife. His brother told me, "I really had no idea that you existed." That hurt me at the time. Why didn't my Father feel I was worth mentioning to his only brother? God, my parents are a piece of work!

We managed to meet a few times before my Mother and Clyde found out and when they did, they were not pleased.

I remember coming home to Mother's house one night and being greeted at the door by Clyde. "Your mother and I want to have a word with you, Fatima," he said, and then led me to the den, where Mother was waiting. We sat down.

"We found out that your father lives here now," said Clyde, "and we don't think you should be going over to see him."

I was stunned, absolutely stunned. Into my silence, Mother spoke.

"Fatima, you're barred from going over to see him. I also don't want you telling him our new address. That's not his place to know."

Clyde took out a letter and handed it to me and said, "We are not saying you cannot see him. I've drawn up this list of conditions under which you can visit him."

My blood was boiling. I could not believe what I was hearing. That son of a bitch had lost it. What a control freak! Thank God I had said no when he asked to adopt me and change my last name. My sister had no choice, but I said no. Who the hell did he think he was?

Clyde handed me the letter. I snatched it out of his hand and kept it as evidence to show what kind of people they really are. I had my evidence. I knew people did not believe me when I told them what I was going through, but this piece of paper was proof. I decided I will keep it forever.

"You can't stop me from seeing my father!" I shouted back.

"Now listen, young lady," started Clyde, but I stood up in a fury.

"I am twenty years old and you are not my father," I shouted back. Clyde shrank down, and Mother stood up, but I shouted at her as well before she could say anything. "You can't tell me what to do anymore and I am so glad that I am leaving this damn house!" This was the second time my mother called me a manipulative bitch.

I stormed back to my room and slammed the door. I took a few deep breaths to calm down. Neither of them followed me and I don't remember us talking any more about it afterwards. Like many of the past confrontations, the explosions came and went, and life resumed.

Not long after, I was finally out of the house and moved in with my aunt and uncle. I still kept my job at Bi-Way on Fridays and Saturdays. I also kept returning to Mother's house on weekends to clean, even though I was no longer living there. I could have said no, I suppose, but there was still a sense of contributing to the family that was a big part of me.

Mother never showed any gratitude when I came. I would ask for a ride to the subway station on Sunday evenings, because buses took longer, and she'd suck her teeth. "I have better things to do with my time than drive you to the train station every week." I suddenly found myself saying, "Fine, in that case, I'll take the bus back on Saturday when I finish work." She looked at me and said nothing. I learned now that I was no longer under her rule as a child, and that if she put up a fuss whenever I asked her for help, I would just find a way to do it myself. No way was I going to give her the satisfaction of holding anything else against me.

I had started to date someone and he would pick me up from work and drop me from home to Mother's place. He said good night and drove off before I opened the front door. My key was not working. I rang the doorbell for a very long time and no one came to the door. They had changed the locks. Those fuckers had changed the locks. A few weeks prior to this, my Mother had sat me down to tell me I need to show Clyde more respect and to say hello when I see him. She said, "she watches to see if I move my lips when I see him. I have a key to the house for which he pays the mortgage." I couldn't take it anymore and told her: "before you met him, you had a condo, and a car, and you didn't need him. He does nothing for me, even though I cook for him and clean up after him." I was livid! I had given her my childhood, I never got into trouble, I did what she told me and I could never, ever make her happy.

They locked me out! I had nowhere to go. I bet he is in front of the television, sitting on his fat ass, grinning ear to ear. That bastard! I hated him.

I slept in the car that night. I didn't go to to work the next day, and instead I went and hung out with my boyfriend before heading back to Scarborough.

My aunt knew the struggles I'd had with my mother. She even remembered the time she threw my sister's shoe at my head during one of our visits to her house. If it had hit me, it wouldn't have been pretty. "I don't understand," she said to Mother, "why do you take your frustrations out on Fatima all the time? It's not necessary." Mother said nothing.

My aunt encouraged me to write a letter to my mother explaining how I felt about our relationship. It seemed like a great idea, so I did. It did not go well. "You are so ungrateful!" Mother shouted at me after reading it. "Do you know the struggles I had with you when you were a baby? Why else do you think I sent you to live with your grandmother?"

"I was in my twenties," and she hadn't stopped using this story to manipulate me, to keep me small, and to make me afraid to stand up for myself against her verbal abuses.

This would be the last time my Mother and I fought. She was so angry that I was seeing my father. When I first met my Father we were both living in Barbados at the same time. The more I thought about it, the more I was sure that she had intentionally kept us apart. She hated him as much as she hated me apparently. I now saw that every time she looked at my face, she saw him.

My interactions with my mother over the next 9 years were minimal. She had actively cut me out of the family. I didn't get invites to family functions of any kind: day trips, birthday parties, vacations… you name it. What my mother did not realize is that she also put distance between my sister and I. I loved my sister and now she was gone.

PREP TIME

Chapter Seven

Men! You can't live with them and you can't live without them. So why bother? Probably because we can't help ourselves. As women we're addicted to how they stir up the thunder between our thighs, the rush of that first kiss from a new pair of lips, their firm grip, their smell and the fantasy of "could he be the one?" For the most part, every man we ever meet prepares us for the next. If we are lucky enough, they feel the same way about us, as we do about them and keep coming back for more. Alas, there comes a time in a woman's life when she needs to put the brakes on, create her ground rules and make a mental checklist of what works and does not work. With every man that came and went, I started to create a database in my mind that recorded the pros and cons in order to pinpoint what it was I wanted and didn't want in a partner. What failed me is that there's a lingering virus of a generational curse hidden from my view, lurking in the background, colouring every decision I made. I could only compare the men I met, to the men I knew. The men of my mother, my grandfather, my father, all had one thing in common; they never showed me any love.

For three years, I lived in Scarborough, looking after my little cousins and finishing up my college diploma in Business Administration. My aunt and uncle started getting territorial. Suddenly, kitchen shelf space was a cause for fights "Don't put your things there! That's ours. You take up too much space!" We also bickered over chores and rent. Suddenly, nothing I did was good enough.

Things were uncomfortable and I felt like I did not belong. All my life I was a tenant in someone else's home; bound to their rules. I did what I was told, I followed what was to be done, but rarely did anyone even so much as say thank you. It was draining and I knew I'd come to a point in my life where I needed independence. I wanted my own space and most of all I had to do this for me.

I spent that last year of living with them saving up as much money as I could. I kept working at Bi-Way until I landed an entry level position at IBM. That bump in pay was just enough for me to move out on my own. At the end of that third year, I packed up my things, found a place with a friend from college, and moved out. I was 22 years old. Funny enough it was my mother who co-signed for us to be able to rent the apartment.

Man, the professional world was not kind to me in that first year! I joined IBM because I wanted to have a very high paying, stable job with all the benefits, just like Mother had taught me. What I had was good, but not great. Problem was, every high paying job needed a basic university degree.

One thing I learned early on was that living a rich, full life doesn't necessarily mean you have to have a fat bank account...but it definitely helps! For the professional positions I wanted, it seemed that Ryerson Polytechnic, in downtown Toronto, offered the programs that I needed.

The funny thing about life is that sometimes it goes full circle. Before this, I hadn't lived enough years on the planet to experience it. Then suddenly, here I was, at 23 years old, starting a four year undergraduate program at a university, and leaving behind my contract spot at IBM to work odd jobs until I could qualify for their higher paying ones. I worked out a deal with IBM to work Friday nights and weekends.

***

I went from rules, rules, rules to girls just wanna have fun! YES! I was single, free, living on my own and you can imagine how different one's dating life can be when you don't have your mother down the hallway! Having my own space, I could walk around naked and free, in my own bedroom of course. I was singing in the shower, spending extra time gliding that cocoa butter all over my skin and this is when I really began to look at myself in the mirror. Paying attention to my body, my curves, as my mind would quickly drift to mysterious moments fantasizing of what was in store for this girl.

One never really knows the rules of dating world. And as much as one appreciates the pleasures that come along with it, dating was work! As excited as I would get to meet new men, to go out on dates, I also put a lot of time getting myself ready for some of these fools. I mean, what do men have to do? Shit, shower and shave, was the extent of it. How was it, that this was all they needed to do and here I was going from top to bottom to ensure my body was clean, smooth and damn fine! I took pride in myself. From ensuring my toes were done, soles of my feet smooth and my body smelling like fresh daisies in every crevice. These were things that were important to me and I eventually got into a rhythm. I called it "prep time". I had to plan in my prep time and depending on the kind of date, and who it was, my prep time was always different. If I liked him, I prepared myself with the fine details, if I was not sure, he got the granny panties.

I would say one of my first adult like relationships was my boyfriend in college. But, just before I started university I broke it off. Over the next 4 years I dated, but never got into a serious relationship. I went out on many dates and had fun and created a lot of lasting friendships. This was an exciting, fun and free time in my life. The time when a woman can really discover what she wants, and doesn't want in a lover.

I got reconnected with a boy who I'd had a small crush on when I first met him at sixteen. A mutual friend set us up on a date, and when he showed up at my door, I just about passed out. He had grown up so much! We hung out for the next five years, but nothing ever came of it. In the back of my mind

I didn't really trust him as I new he had a girlfriend, and I was afraid that if we got together, in the end he'd choose her and I'd be left out in the cold. At least, that was my belief, a belief that I now see might have been related to my grandfather's behaviour, and my memory of it.

Once, I met a lawyer from upstate New York. Ha! Now he was fun! He came to visit me often, and I went to visit him once, for American Thanksgiving. Nothing ever came of our dating, though. He was 32 and wanted to settle down, and I was still in my twenties loving the single life. I really wasn't into long distance relationships, either: they cost too much money in travel and phone bills. That's how I first discovered that one of my core relationship needs was that my man must be local. Last I heard, my lawyer friend had gotten a job in Manhattan just before 9/11, and I have always wondered what happened to him.

At Ryerson, I met a gentleman who hung out with me all the time, like my best friend. We would watch Oprah together at my place or over the phone, do homework and projects together. He liked to cook and smelled good. Nothing ever came of that because after three years of knowing he was living with a female roommate, it finally hit me that they were more than friends when I had the 'pleasure' of listening to them make out when he thought he had hung up the phone.'

I even met a white guy who my family called the "Italian Stallion" because his family was from Italy. I dated him for a while, but what kept stopping me from taking it further was a single question: how much would my family disapprove if we married? Would I be able to take him back to Barbados? On the other side of the coin, I also knew his family would not approve of me. We were a couple for about a week, then I called it off because I was not comfortable in my own skin. In my heart of hearts, I didn't truly believe that he could really like me. I was a black woman who believed from an early age that white boys didn't like black woman, especially this one. Nor, I wasn't about do the whole "Jungle Fever" thing.

The last casual guy I remember dating was a man I met at a club. He was cute, but I could not understand a word that came out his mouth because he had a heavy Jamaican accent. When we spoke on the phone, my roommate would listen on the other end and translate. He spoke patois and for the life of me he sounded like he was speaking riddles. I would just say yes to everything and who the hell knows what I was saying yes too. I promised to call him back, but it was two weeks before I remembered. By then, his phone number was no longer stored in the phone. Funny thing: he never called me back, either.

I began to go to church again. This time it was different as it was something that I wanted to do. It was calling me. Regardless of how uncomfortable I felt with some of the church goers, that was a place where I knew God was speaking to me. The sermons spoke to my heart and they cleared my mind. Most people avoided church because it was forced down their throats as a kid, however my experience was opposite. No one would take me and no one would tell me why. It was only in my early teens that this part of my life began. It would come in and out of my life, but no matter what, for me church was in my heart, in my head and God was always with me. I began to style my hair naturally, and only wore dresses and skirts because that was the dress code. It was at this time that I got baptised in the Apostolic faith. I attended church twice on Sundays, Bible study on Wednesdays, and learned a lot of things that today I can't even remember. Carlin started calling and wanting to hang out but I could never trust him as he was always in and out of my life and in and out of some kind of life issue or crisis. So one time I just invited him to church and bible study. He came and I thought that was a good sign, however one of the Bible Study teacher's told me after meeting that he was not the right one for me. What did he know? He knows nothing of our friendship. I just left it open to see how the whole Carlin thing would pan out. And of course nothing came of it because he disappeared again!

A few things had changed, of course. I was living on my own, a grown-ass woman without anyone to tell her what to do, what to eat, or who to date. I had responsibilities...but it was all about new beginnings. It was the best time of my life.

And that wasn't the only thing that went full circle.

Two years into my studies, I found myself at the Eaton Centre food court. I remember that it was warmer, a Saturday in March when the deep freeze of the winter had lifted from the city and you could feel the first traces of spring in the air. Crowds of shoppers surged passed me in light jackets and bags as I took the escalators down to the food court to get some lunch.

The burger place downstairs had a line-up it, so I got in. Standing there, I looked around, idly watching the people around me. My eyes rested on two people sitting at a table. I looked at the man, a younger guy, very lean and chiseled, wearing a beige turtleneck sweater, plain blue jeans and running shoes.

Hmm, I thought, he kind of looks like Ron from school.

I couldn't turn my attention back to the line as we slowly made our way forward.

No...it was Ron! Oh my God!

He'd gotten older, had trimmed his Afro down a bit. As I lived and breathed, Ronald Gould had grown up. He looked good! I didn't recognize the woman he was with, but they were skinning' and grinning' and seemed really happy. I broke out of the line and walked over to them.

"Ron?" I asked as I approached. Ron looked over, and frowned for a second before he recognized me.

"Fatima Devonish? Oh my God, how are you?" He got up and hugged me. Immediately: flashes of that night in the hallway, his arms, his kiss.....and then I snapped back to reality.

"I've been great! I just finished my third year at Ryerson!"

"Oh yeah?" said Ron. "And to think you used to call me "nerd"!"

I smirked. "You're still a nerd. What are you up to these days?"

Ron leaned back. "Oh, not much. Still living around here, playing some music, working odd jobs. It's a good life."

"I can see that." I paused. The woman he was with was smiling politely, but Ron didn't have to introduce her because I recognized her from high school. We used to hang out with her older brother. We also went to the same church in high school and had the same friends. The moment suddenly turned awkward. There was a pregnant silence as I suddenly felt like the third wheel.

"Well," I said, "it was good to see you again. Best of luck!"

Ron smiled. "The same to you!"

And just like that, I walked away. After I'd gone about thirty seconds, I thought, maybe I should go back and give him my number. But that would have been strange with her there. I had no idea if they were a thing or not, but as I kept on walking back to my food lineup, I wondered about that meeting, especially at this time in my life. What a coincidence, to see him again now. I could not believe that was who he ended up with.

Oh well. I truly hoped he was happy and maybe it was for the best. But somehow I felt I had lost my second chance.

All these years I always remembered his birthday. His name would be a separate blessing that I would pray for out of all the other prayers I would make. And I would wonder, within the little breaks in the stream of consciousness of everyday living, how was Ron doing? What was he up to? Has life been good to him?

But at no point in that time did I ever speak to Ron, or meet up with him. However he would always remain my hero.

***

Carlin reappeared in my life around the time I was working at Sprint Canada after graduating from Ryerson with a degree in Administration and Information Management and landing my first real full-time job.

During my last year at Ryerson, I was going to church regularly, and I decided that maybe Carlin did deserve another shot. For the last 17 years he had come in and out of my life. He had been a great friend but when he would vanish it would hurt me so much. Yet every time he reappeared I would let him back in.

For several weeks at church I was hearing different stories and sermons about forgiveness and love. Therefore, I had to consider that I had missed having a deeper friendship with him.

What's more, Carlin had always supported me getting along with Mother, always had my back when it came to my own growth. I wouldn't even have gone to Ryerson were it not for his advice. And Carlin was a little romantic, too. It was fun heading out to Scarborough Town Centre on two dollar movie dates with him. Almost each time, there was a moment when he'd look at me with friendly eyes and say "You're pretty".

Carlin accepted me for who I was. The question was, could I accept him for who he was? Somewhere, the sweet 14 year old kid, the one I had known before all of these complications, was still inside this 28 year old man.

Finally, after 17 years of saying no, I finally said yes.

At first, Carlin and I took it slow. We took the time to get to know each other a little better as grownups. We'd go away for long weekend trips to Windsor, Niagara Falls, and Montreal. We'd eat and explore the sights, and just relax in the hotel rooms and talk and laugh for hours on end. It was a carefree time, so much fun, and with zero worries.

I let the walls down, little by little. At one point, we went in on a car together, I helped him buy a car under my name while he made the payments and insurance.

We got along very well, and at the time, I started having thoughts that this man would be the one with whom I would finally start a family. We began to date and see one another a lot. We became very close and one day out of the blue he said:

"Fatima, we should get married. What do you say?" At the time, I said "yes" thinking we may just be playing around. After all, it made sense. Why not get married with the one person who's already proven they're there for you? He may have come in and out of my life, yet for the most part, there was some consistency with him.

The marriage never happened. Carlin and I lived in what I call "blissful sin", doing everything that other married couples did, but without the wedding rings. Nevertheless, I made the decision to stick with the person who I had known since I was 14 years old, a friend for half my life at that point. Now, at 28 years old, he wanted to have children. The catch was, I was planning to move to Barbados.

"But what will happen to me?" he said one day when he called me up to chat.

"What about you?" I replied. "Unless you're planning to move to Barbados, too, I can't help you."

For two years, we stood in that holding pattern, as I worked and pondered a way that I could make the move. We dated, hung out, and talked about our plans for the future, but I still held back. In the back of my mind lurked the reality of Carlin's secret girlfriend, the one that I had asked him about back when we were seeing each other the first time, the woman he's dismissed as "just a friend". Same girl that ended up being the mother of his daughter. Same girl who seemed to show up at every single family gathering that I got invited to.

Part of me believed that a tiger never changes his stripes. Another part wanted to give him a second chance.

***

The first red flag came when his daughter's mother called my house one day.

"Could I speak to Carlin, please?" she asked.

Hmm…how had she gotten my number? Immediately, my mind went back to his secret girlfriends. No, Carlin couldn't be messing around with me again. I looked over to the bed where he lay snoring quietly, having stayed over the night before.

"He's asleep," I said, "Can I get him to phone you back later?"

A brief pause right before an annoyed "sure", then she hung up.

I hung up the phone and stood for a moment. I was annoyed, but the feeling faded. Things were going well, this was just a hiccup

The second red flag, and the one that changed everything, happened a few weeks later, when a different woman called. This time, she was more agitated.

"Where is Carlin? I really need to speak with him."

"Carlin's away right now," I said, "and you know, this isn't really his number. You should try calling him directly if you want to talk to him."

Bitter sounding chuckle from the other end of the phone. "I guess I should wait until his next visit, then."

My gut felt like it had dropped down to the ground. "What….what do you mean?"

"What do you think? He's still having sex with me. He's having sex with both of us, and you know what? This is bullshit!"

I didn't respond for a few seconds while I processed the shock. "How long has this been going on?'

"I don't know! A while!"

"Has it been months or a year?"

Then, before she could answer, I hung up the phone. I didn't want to know. It didn't matter.

That fucker...he lied to me again!! What a fool I am. Why do I do this to myself? Just like that, I broke it off with Carlin, and rebuilt that wall around my heart once again. I was done. Enough of Carlin… ENOUGH!!

Faith Of A Mustard Seed

Chapter Eight

Hardships prepare you to expand who you are. They can be filled with pain, yet they can also be a source of pleasure. What I do know is that when life threw me pain, I found peace in God's presence. Faith is something hard to describe, even harder to have. With faith everything is possible, but for many there is disbelief. "Doubt your doubts, but don't doubt God!" is a statement that guides me when I want to give up, when I want to give in and, most of all, when I simply don't give a shit. Faith is the one thing that every human being has access to, regardless of race or religion. It is free, powerful and the one gift we are given that has the ability to give those moments when you just want to give up, lock the door and throw away the key, another fighting chance.

***

Before long, November 9, 1996 finally dawned. It was time for me to head back to Barbados.

I made my way to Pearson Airport and boarded the plane with the same bittersweet sense of purpose and sadness that I was once again leaving loved ones behind. I remember the excitement and anticipation on that five hour flight, watching out the window as the snow and ice of the North American soil below gave way to the vibrant green and pale blue waters of the Caribbean. But funny enough, I cried like a baby at the airport. Canada had long become my home and had given me many opportunities. What was I about to give up by leaving it all behind? And yet, the truth was that I could use some distance from Canada, the cold weather and the disappointments of my childhood. There was something down there for me, and me alone, and I wanted to claim it.

All of it was worth it when the plane finally touched down. To this day, I remember the smell of the air when the plane came to a stop on the tarmac and the doors opened. It was the smell of home in my heart. Electricity, that galvanizing odor that for Canadians tends to happen in the summertime right before a thunderstorm. That's the smell of Barbados.

The best part was looking up at the crowds of Bajans near customs waiting with name signs welcoming their loved ones… and then seeing my cousins waiting for me with big smiles on their faces. My heart burst at seeing them as I embraced them. I knew that I had come back home and had come back for good.

So much had changed. Evelyn and my Aunt Baby had passed away from cancer. My cousins were now grown up and had children of their own. My entire set of childhood friends had moved to Canada or the USA. The beach; however, remained the same.

None of that truly mattered to me. I was now back to being part of a life that had ended the moment I got on board the plane to Toronto with Baby two decades earlier. I was back home and loving every minute of it!

When I heard news that Toronto got hit by its first big snowstorm that January, I was lounging enjoying 30 degree temperatures.

Funny things started to happen while I was there, things that never happened back home. For one thing, Mother, my sister and my father called me more often. Sometimes, they would all call me on the same day. "Why do you guys always call me so close to each other?" I asked them on one such day. Each of them gave their own version of the same answer: "You're too far away now and we just want to check up on you, see how you're doing." Who knew they cared so much? Being apart from Mother and my sister for so many years, I had convinced myself that I really did not have a close family. I mean Mother and I seldom interacted over the past 9 years. Now I am gone and she acts like we're best friends. It confused me, but I let it go and enjoyed all the attention I was getting.

Lying is a choice, not a mistake. When I decided to move to Barbados and leave Carlin behind after having two women call, he kept on contacting me. I did not understand what was going on in his head. He could look at me, straight in my face all that time, knowing he was poking some other puss and always coming back to me. I know I was his comfort zone, his safety net. I was his friend and not just another piece of ass. Carlin called me every other day, always asking the same question: "When are you coming home? I miss you." Did he think those three words were going to make a difference? He kept on coming in and out of my life, he lied, he cheated and now he was acting like he was sorry. And for some reason he believed that no matter what, I would change my mind. I will admit it, I did like the attention. I was getting attention from everywhere! My family from Barbados seemed happy that I was there. My parents and sister were the ones reaching out to me, and Carlin, well he just would not give up. I was home at last and life was good.

My Aunt's husband had a job, at my workplace, and I spent a lot of time getting to know her and her family. I was making good money to cover my expenses. My Uncle Conliffe and his family had me over for their functions, and I got to enjoy all the delicious and spicy home cooked meals that I'd missed while I was in Canada. This was truly the best time of my life.

While blizzards and snowstorms created whiteout conditions back in Toronto, I got to take in the vivid greens, bright pink and yellow flowering plants lining the road along the airport as I headed for my family's home in Weston, St. James, to the familiar calypso pink walled house.

It took me two weeks to get a job. My experience, up to that point, was as a help desk analyst, taking calls from customers who were experiencing difficulties with their computers. In Barbados, there was a position open at a

Barbados Telecommunications Company. I threw my hat in and got the job! What an opportunity! To get a job working for one of the best companies on the Island and I had done it on my own!!! I was proud of myself.

***

Just before I left Toronto, I was diagnosed with asthma. One of the things that people do in the Caribbean is burn their yard waste and newspapers in open pits behind their homes. Going about my day, whenever I'd pass by one of those fires, that thick smoky smell caused me to start wheezing. I went to the doctors and was given a puffer to carry around with me because I was a citizen and the puffers were free. The asthma, though, wasn't nearly as bad as when I started lactating. This was even stranger considering that I wasn't even pregnant.

I had no clue what this was, but between the asthma and the lactation, I had this rippling chest pain every time I took a breath. One day, it happened on the job, and someone drove me to the hospital, where they took some x-rays. Before leaving Canada, I'd known I had a fibroid, so I assumed that must have been it. When I told the doctor, at a private clinic to check it out, he came back with a complete surprise.

"Miss Devonish," he said, "it's not a fibroid that you have, it's a tumour in your uterus. You'll need to have it operated on. Now, that's not a procedure we do at this facility. You'll need to go to a private hospital not far from here. They'll take care of the operation and you can recover there."

"Okay… how much will it cost to do this surgery?" I asked him.

"I can't say for certain until we go through with it," the doctor replied, "but you can count on it being around the $3,000 mark, which includes a one-week bed fee for your post-op. If you recover faster, we can refund you the difference."

"Well, are you a surgeon?"

"Yes."

"What's your fee?"

The doctor grinned. "We'd have to put you on a payment plan."

I raised my eyebrow. "Payment plan? Are you serious? Okay…"

"If we go in," the doctor continued, "we'd first have to do an exploratory surgery to see the condition of the tumour. If removal is called for, then we would perform a hysterectomy right on the spot. You'd never be able to have children." What was interesting about that whole procedure was that at no point was there an ultrasound. Instead, he simply touched my stomach with his hands; no other tests. Can you say "quack"?

I didn't do it. Something about the procedure and the diagnosis didn't make sense to me. I'd never had a doctor tell me that I could lose the ability to have children as a result of this tumour. The clincher came when I talked to my relatives, with whom I was staying with, about what was happening. When I mentioned the private hospital in question, my aunt said "Oh lord, you don't want to go there! You guh die! That's what happens at that hospital."

When I got my bill for the visit a few days later, it amounted to $270 and change. I suddenly found myself missing the Canadian healthcare system. I decided to head back to Toronto and find out from my old gynecologist what was happening.

I took two weeks off, in May of 1997, and flew back to Toronto. When I met with my gyno, she took a look and refused to operate. When I insisted, she sighed. "Fatima, you're a little too young for this kind of procedure, which is why I'm hesitant. If you do insist on surgery, of course, we'll go in and do what we can to remove the growth; however, if we see there's too much bleeding, I may have to give you a full hysterectomy."

"Would you have to wake me up to ask me first?" I asked.

She shook her head. "No. For that type of bleeding, we can't risk delaying that decision. You'd simply wake up and it would be over."

That seemed fishy to me. In my mind, I was thinking: "Can you say Quack Doctor Number Two?"

I decided to get a third opinion. This doctor came back and explained it in a sensible way that neither of the previous two doctors had bothered to do.

"Fatima," he said, "your fibroid is as big as a grapefruit and I don't recommend taking it out because of where it is. I saw it on the outside of your uterus, not on the inside. When they grow inside of a uterus, the egg can't implant and there would be no baby. The baby and the fibroid are going to fight for space, and you'll have excruciating pain and either the baby will win or the fibroid will win. The baby cuts off the blood flow to the fibroids, and then you start having pain, which could lead to a miscarriage."

He took a breath before saying the next part. "Are you married?"

I shook my head. "No!"

"If you want to have children," he said, "now's the time."

I walked away from the meeting in a cloud of uncertainty and anxiety. Did I really want children? I hadn't entertained the question that much throughout my life. Like other young people, I just assumed it was something in my future and left it at that, a concept. Now, I was at a true crossroads. In one direction, a life of solitude in which I grew old with no little ones to raise. In the other, a life in which I could demonstrate that I could be a far better mother to my own children than my Mother had been to me on some level.

I explored my feelings and the pangs of regret and fear rising up in my chest, convinced me. I was however, glad that I had completed my education. If need be, I would be able to raise children. How hard could it be, I thought? My mother and grandmother seemed to do well by it.

Now, in order to have children, I needed a man. The only man in my life that I would even consider having a child with was Carlin. His charm, his daily calls to me saying he missed me, and the fact that for 17 years of my life he was pretty much the most consistent thing, had me think, okay if I need to have kids, he would most likely be the one. Besides no matter what, I felt some level of comfort and love for him.

Not long after that appointment, I met up with Carlin and I explained to him everything the doctor had said to me. He listened carefully, nodded his understanding, until I got to the very last statement.

"Carlin," I said as I finished, "I want to have children."

Carlin was quiet for a few minutes. Then he spoke. "Okay. We'll figure it out."

I smiled at him, and in that moment, he leaned over and kissed me, as he took me in his arms. It felt good, and safe, being held by an old friend, and the soon-to-be father of my children.

I stayed in Toronto after that, dropping all of my plans to move to Barbados. It was a bittersweet decision. Someday soon, I'll live my dream of moving to back to Barbados to live there before I die.

Mostly, I stayed because Carlin was here. He was the only man I knew for so many years that was consistently kind and caring. Yes, he was an ass and had come in and out of my life, but no matter what, he always came back. I had nothing to measure against, in terms of what it looked like to be with the right man. All I knew was that I never had a father figure in my life. I knew men in one way: they weren't around and when they were, they were ass holes and control freaks. My greatest experience of a man was Ron and well, Ron and I were kids when we met. I can't expect to find a grown man who'll be my knight in shining armour like Ron had way back then. That wasn't realistic. Carlin was the best man I knew, regardless of his lies and the other women, he always came back to me and I knew he loved me, despite his fucked up ways. I had known him forever and a day. I could always trust him to want to be around me and I did love him. Why not let him be the person that I start my family with? Within two weeks of my permanent return, I got a new job and I was back at my aunt's home in Scarborough. I was spending my nights with Carlin at his mother's place.

I quickly gathered that Carlin's mother was not too happy about it, and made it known to him, and to me! She would pick at me every time I crossed her path. If it wasn't my clothes, it was my hair or how ugly I was. I had no idea what her issue was and I never asked. I just knew it was about her son and not me. Soon after, at family functions, some of Carlin's other relatives started to pick on me too. I just ignored them.

***

I had gone for a routine check up on my fibroids. The moment the doctor said the words "you're pregnant," my life transformed forever. January 6, 1998 was the day my heart swelled with joy. I was going to a mom.

As scared as I was, I was in love with this child I hadn't even met. A life was growing inside of me. I dreamed of being a mother. I promised God that I would love my kids and never do to them what was done to me. I was carrying this blessing, in my body, and no matter what the doctors warned me about, I had faith. I had God. I had my heavenly father's promise that if I have faith the size of a mustard seed, I'd be able to see the mountaintop and He shall be there.

It was unreal. I was now responsible for two lives: my own and the one growing inside of me. As scary as it felt, it was also a love unlike anything I had experienced. So I began my lifelong commitment to my son. Without the doctor having to tell me, I just knew, and felt, it was a boy.

"What shall we do now?" I asked Carlin when I told him the news. He was surprised, but also ready with a plan.

"We're going to have the baby and move in together," he said. "Let's get a condo instead of renting. It's a better investment. We'll just have to get the 5% down on a place before September." September 3, 1998 was when the baby was due, according to the doctors.

It was scary at first having this living presence inside of my body. The strange dreams, the odd cravings and the aches and pains of carrying a small human. But I was a survivor and I was going to be a tough ass bitch with this challenge as with all of the others.

If I was going to live with Carlin however, there were a few conditions that I needed established in order to feel safe. For starters, he had to quit smoking by the time the baby arrived. For another, there would be no messing around on his part. This was a deal breaker. I did not want to deal with anymore crazy women calling me up to give me crap. He agreed to all of these and we went ahead with our plans.

During those nine months, I moved from my aunt's house to live with Carlin's sister, who was dating my cousin, at the time. That decision had its moments of fun along with many challenges. We found a condo in May. God, how free it was to walk into that empty space, with the key in hand, knowing that it was ours! Our friends and family all came together to help us set up for the baby. It was a time of such promise.

As the doctors had predicted, five months into the pregnancy, I was wracked with intense pain as the baby began to battle the fibroid for nutrients in a fight to the death. I was briefly hospitalized and I prayed for my son to win his struggle. During this time, Carlin would sometimes disappear for a long time. I didn't think anything of it at the time despite his history. People need their space after all, and we were in a stressful situation. I supposed he just didn't like being around my family.

Towards the end of my pregnancy, I was told I had only gained 11 pounds. That was not enough weight gain, and they began to wonder if the child had developed normally. Still, there was a quiet awareness inside me that everything was fine.

On September 3rd, as planned, I went into labour, knowing that my life would never be the same again. On that day, Carlin was there every step of the way. Together, we became parents.

"Don't be afraid," Ma told me, "because at the end of the pain and pushing, you'll have a child." I kept her words in my mind throughout the painful birthing process.

Ultimately, she was right. I have learned that pain is the teacher of the lesson in understanding pleasure. You cannot really understand one without the other. Giving birth is one of the truest of miracles; a miracle that unfolds before our eyes over 9 months. A combination of fear, joy and uncertainty culminating in the welcoming of a new person into our often crazy, rarely predictable lives. It is an act of courage and selflessness that, in the end, gives birth to a new life. There he was. I had seen him before he was born. I knew he was coming, no matter what! Even when the doctors said it would be a big risk, I knew he was there, growing inside of me and now here he was, my healthy 7 pound, 8 ounce baby boy. Oh God, thank you! He was all mine. My baby boy.

THE IRREFUTABLE SIGN

Chapter 9

I believe that God gives us signs to move onto the next chapter of our lives. We may not like them, but they are there. They become obvious to us when we pay attention. I have learned the hard way that by not following those signs, we end up causing damage to ourselves. We live in a big universe filled with energy. We are all made up of this energy, which has us all connected, and for me God is at the source of it all. There is a power beyond us that we may not understand, but to deny its existence, is to rob ourselves of the presence of God's blessings in our life.

Throughout my life, I have spent many days and nights crying. My circumstances overdressed with pain. My pain paralyzing me with uncertainty, lead by fear. A rollercoaster of ups and downs leaving me dizzy with confusion and doubt. There were so many times when I would cry out to my heavenly father and say, "I don't get it God, but I know you do. I want to be thankful for this opportunity but I'm not, it's too hard. I ask you to please help me let it go so I can move on."

So there I was, I had just turned 30 and I was holding my son. His little body tightly wrapped in his blue blanket, pressing against my breast. I knew he was falling asleep to the rhythm of my heart beat. Each time I would look down at his precious face, I would stare in wonder. I thought: this is too good to be true. And then I would stop myself and say "No Fatima, you asked God for this" and God had answered! His timing sucks at times, and what I pray for does not always come when I want it, but I either get what I pray for or something greater comes along. So in fact God's timing is perfect, even when not aligned with mine! Nothing in the world could have been a greater gift than my son.

There are things no one told me about having a baby. First, your stomach does not go back down right away. I learned that one very quickly. Next, your breasts double in size. Just one day after giving birth, they hurt like a bitch and it was extremely painful to breastfeed. You bleed for nearly a month afterwards. And finally, if a doctor cuts you, you have to sit in a sitz bath every day for a week for the pain.

As a first time mother, no matter how you grow up, no one can really prepare you. For the most part, I could deal with everything else. These were just surprises I never knew about and could have done without.

For the first six weeks, everything was good. It was pretty much the same routine everyday. Mother and son were doing well and every check up came back normal. The only complaint I had was not getting enough sleep. I fed the baby every three hours day and night. I really felt like I was missing something, but just could not put my finger on it.

The after effects of childbirth were starting to take their toll on me. I became anxious, which caused Carlin and I to bicker constantly. My brain would go foggy. I would have an out of body experience and start yelling at him for the littlest of things: not cleaning the bathroom, helping with the laundry or neglecting to make the bed in morning. After one such incident I locked eyes with him, with a firm arrogant tone and asked, "How the hell do you expect me to remember every damn thing that goes on here? Can't you see I have other things to do?!"

Carlin's eyes went wide and he stormed away. He was in shock and so was I. Where the hell did that come from? I sounded like Mother yelling at Clyde. Dear Lord, I felt sick. Who was that bitch? Was that me? I was holding my son in my arms when that rage came out of me. I didn't recognize who I was and I certainly didn't know what was wrong with me.

A day or two passed, we didn't talk about it so I couldn't apologize. Instead, I kept to myself. I was tired, miserable and feeling really guilty, not only for snapping at Carlin, but also for being unhappy. God has blessed me with this beautiful baby and I'm not happy! Why am I not happy?

I was aware of how I was behaving and yet it did not stop me. The mood swings continued. My God, it wasn't pretty! I was just angry and irritable all the time. I ended up going on the pill on my doctor's advice, with a plan to wait another four years before having a second child. Still, I would forget to take it from time to time. I didn't want to get fat on the pill, which was one of the side effects, but ended up eating an entire apple pie and a carton of ice cream every two days or so.

After about three months of not being able to take the pill regularly, I switched to shots every three months. I had heard bad things about IUDs, so that was not an option.

After my second injection I began to notice a bald spot on my head. Oh God, what was this! My hair was falling out! I started to comb it over every morning, but I couldn't hide it, especially not from Carlin.

"Don't worry," he said, "it'll grow back." I didn't believe him.

I started waking up in fear, tired from having to feed the baby every three hours like clockwork, even through the night. I was doing housework, during the day, before Carlin came home, and making dinner for us both. Carlin did very little by comparison. It made sense to me: if he was the one working all day, I should at least take care of the house. I figured he'd step up his game once I found work again. When I went to my doctor with these emotional symptoms, she said I was likely suffering from postpartum depression and offered me some treatment options.

Back then the word "Postpartum" was not really used. Many women would suffer shame in silence. When a woman had a baby she was supposed to be happy as she had just been blessed, yet we cannot always control the science of our bodies. Carlin thought I was going crazy and so did I at times. But

I knew this was not me and decided not to take the antidepressant pills. I just had to trust that this too shall pass. Eventually things got better and we were managing okay. It seemed to me that Carlin and I were getting closer as a couple.

We became so close that a few years later I was pregnant again. December 7th, 2000 my baby girl was born. The children were 28 months apart and it was a very busy time. A toddler in one hand and a newborn in the other. Life had really begun for me. I was a Mother. A mother of two beautiful children. I had my own family. I felt that I had lived up to my mother's expectations of what a good, successful life was. A stable job with benefits, a supportive common law husband, a simple home and children of my own. I had come to believe that these were things I wanted for myself as well, and they certainly were.

As much as I was grounded in knowing I had a family of my own and my children were my world, I could no longer turn a blind eye to what was happening around me. As one day rolled into the next, so did the stress of our relationship. I do not recall a single incident that started to make it go downhill, but it did quickly.

***

Now, I always knew that Carlin drank, that was just something that was so.

As far back as when we were kids, I knew this was true. His family always drank, mostly beer and some hard liquor. Carlin had been smoking cigarettes since the age of 16. I knew about this for most of our twenties, but since I wasn't involved with him, it didn't really matter to me. He could drink and smoke all he wanted.

When we did get involved, though, and we were moving in, I had to talk to him about it. "The thing about it is," I said, "if you're going to continue to smoke and drink, we can't be together. That's not the kind of environment I want to live in."

"I understand," Carlin replied. "That's fine, I can stop. I care more about you than any drink, anyway."

He didn't stop.

When we found out I was pregnant the first time, Carlin promised to stop again. "It's really important that we make a clean and safe environment for this baby," I said to him. "You really need to stop with the drinking and smoking, at least for the pregnancy."

Carlin had smiled and tried to reassure me. "Of course," he said. "I'll stop, for the sake of the baby."

He didn't stop.

In the end, I endured it. We were already together and there wasn't much I could do to control it anyway. But Carlin kept breaking his promises. We agreed that he should smoke on the balcony so that the smoke would disperse outside rather than getting concentrated inside the condo. In the summertime, Carlin would declare "man, it's too hot to smoke outside! Can I have a puff in here?" In the wintertime, it was too cold. He knew that I would absolutely not tolerate him smoking in the living room or kitchen, so the bathroom became the smoking room. Even that was a little ridiculous because you could still smell it throughout the house. I was embarrassed to have anybody over. I was always cleaning because I didn't want the bathroom to smell all sooty. It gets black and brown after a while. If anybody in my family came, I would hide everything.

Between drinking and smoking, most people treat smoking as the worse of the two. Strangely, I had a handle on Carlin's habit. But the booze… I never saw it come in, but when it left, it left in a big box. I'd take out the recycling and think, "Where the hell is this man putting all of this?"

Carlin went from drinking Labatt's Maximum King cans to the 7% big bottles. I learnt quickly that this is how you can tell if someone's an alcoholic: they know the alcohol content of everything that they drink before they buy it. He would be drinking 7% beer every day after he came home from work. On the weekends he started at 5 o'clock in the morning. Pretty soon, the alcohol content wasn't enough, so he went from drinking 7% beer and smoking, to 10% Crest beer and smoking that really sends you for a loop. A couple of people that he smoked with said, "I can't drink that beer and smoke because the buzz is too much. You don't know what's going on." On top of that, Carlin would chase 100% overproof rum with Crest 10% beer.

Carlin's habits had a huge impact, but probably nowhere near as strong as on our finances. Despite working two full time jobs in very lucrative positions, we were always in overdraft. It costs a lot to maintain that level of smoking and drinking.

Those arguments took place at some of the lowest points in my life. I felt like crap and I looked like crap. Not long after I had my son, my hair fell out, forcing me to re-style into a comb-over. Not long after that, I cut it off and had a low Afro. I was not comfortable with myself, with my hair or my mind, body and soul. I figured since I did not have a job or the money to pay to get my hair done, this was the cheapest thing to do. I was told it suited my face; however, Carlin did not want me to cut my hair. The comb over made me feel unwanted and unkempt. There was nothing sexy about me at that time. I did not feel like a desirable woman.

I started to wear track pants, track suits, jeans, t-shirts, running shoes and flats; some old type of granny shoes. Carlin, oddly enough, dressed the same way. I started to wear some of his clothes. My cousin came over during that time and looked at me funny. "You are starting to look, act and sound alike," she remarked. "You need to pull yourself together." Carlin's mother would pick at me and call me an "old looking hag." I had no self-worth and low self-esteem.

One time, we were in the bathroom, having a big fight over money. By then, we had decided to share a joint account and it was never enough. In the heat of the moment, Carlin took my hand and twisted it, wrenching it around. It hurt, and though he apologized afterwards, I thought at the time, "Oh man, this is not a good sign."

This was the first of many violent incidents.

The next was when I was three months pregnant with Sarah. We were standing, at the front door, by the closet. Carlin took out his wallet and realized he had no cash on him. "I need the bank card to go to the LCBO," he said. "Can you give me yours?"

I clicked my mouth. "No. You're going to buy more rum? Uh uh, I don't think so. We have the mortgage coming out and the maintenance fee. Groceries too. There's no extra money for your drinking this week, sorry."

Next thing I knew, he pushed me up against the front door. In the process, I tripped on some shoes. Carlin took the bank card and left. When he was gone, I called his brother. "You need to tell your brother to keep his hands off me. No man in my life has ever laid hands on me and you'd better believe he's not going to make this a habit! Who does he think he is?"

One day, not long before I had Sarah, when Carlin was at work, I walked to the police station and sat down with the community officer to find out my options. The officer was very friendly and showed compassion, along with the sternness that comes with the job. After explaining the situation, he sighed. "Well," he said, "if you tell us where you live and we go now, we will remove him and he will never be back. Given your situation, I can understand why you wouldn't necessarily want to do that now, but you should know: once violence starts, it doesn't stop. It will continue to escalate."

I nodded and took in his words. "Okay," I said. "I will consider all of this and let you know. Thanks for your time." I went home and did nothing.

Six months after Sarah was born, I ended up losing my job and Carlin was supporting all of us for the second time. I had also lost my job when Anton was two months old. I thought to myself here we go again. The atmosphere in the house was tense. You never knew with Carlin what would set him off on his next episode. The pattern was the same: we'd have a money crunch, he'd want to go buy something from the liquor store, I'd protest and it turned into a shouting match. I'd then get on the phone with my cousin and encourage them to come over to make sure Carlin didn't get too out of control. Things would cool down and we'd continue from where we left off.

Part of why I didn't take action was that I wanted two kids. That was my vision of an ideal family. This was also a strange time in my life. I never had any money. The way I dressed myself continued to changed, going from always having matching shoes, panties, bras, everything tight and hooked up… to track pants and sweat tops, all the time. I managed to control the issues with my hair by wearing it in braids as it grew back from cutting it off when Anton was 18 months old. I gained a lot of weight. I didn't sleep much, I didn't eat much. I just 'was.' I would wake up with an acidic stomach that was full of anxiety.

By now I was 33 years old. Sarah was born, and around that time Anton had been diagnosed with an asthmatic cough. I believed it was from hanging around all of the smoking that was supposedly kept to the bathroom. It was nonsense! The condo was too small, and after five years of living there, Carlin and I decided we would look for a house.

As I held Sarah in my arms late one night, Carlin snoring on the bed nearby, Anton asleep in his own room, I looked around. This was not the way I wanted to live, but I didn't seem to have a choice. With a young baby and no job, I was entirely dependent on Carlin to survive. That was the moment I decided to ask God for an irrefutable sign: should I take my kids and leave this man?

If I did, how could I leave? Where would I go? "The court will never give you custody without a job," Carlin had warned me after one of our fights.

I started going back to church. My life was spiraling out of control and I decided the way to get everything back in order was to reconnect with God. More than that, I went so I could pray that we could get our relationship back on a good foundation. Maybe we'd get married and finally build the kind of life that we always talked about, the one we would have together with the kids. It wasn't happening of course, so I started to ask for that irrefutable sign. And omen from up high that I simply could not dispute. I closed my eyes, made the request and let it go.

***

After being off work for over a year and the stress of living with Carlin, I decided I needed a break. So, I went to stay with my mother for two weeks. Carlin shrugged it off. I'm not sure how he felt about it, but it didn't matter.

At the same time, my cousin and my sister said they were coming to take me out for dinner in order to come up with a game plan for me. During that time, at my mother's, I had some breathing space away from all of the anxiety and stress. I started to feel alive again.

With this new energy, I decided to start going for job interviews once again. Before long, I'd managed to find an opportunity as a Help Desk Analyst at a transportation and logistics company. The job was perfectly in line with my education and payed very well. The only setback was the rotating shift work: three days of work per week, 12 hours a day, 7am to 7pm, then 7pm to 7am.

"You won't be able to do this by yourself," said Mother. "We'll help you."

When I worked night shifts during the week, Anton and Sarah would go to Mother's house. I'd get them on my way back home from work. We did this for a while, and though it took me eight months, I did eventually get back to a Monday to Friday day shift.

With two incomes now bringing us money, the financial stress largely went away, which somewhat improved things between Carlin and I. We still had our hot and cold moments and I continued to put up with his drinking and smoking.

In the back of my mind though, I continued to work on an exit strategy.

***

A pattern emerged in Carlin's behaviour. Every six weeks, he'd pick a fight with me over something stupid. Then, he'd tell me, "pick up Anton from daycare, I need to go out later."

"Where are you going?" I would ask him.

"Out with the people on the street," he'd say back to me.

I would pick up Anton and Carlin would go out until late at night. When he came back home, he'd be drunk. He reeked of booze and something else that was so rank I was never able to figure out what it was.

A couple of times, Carlin made so much noise coming in that it woke me up. I'd head out to the hallway and I'd see him trying to piss in the closet or on the computer. "What the hell are you doing?" I'd hiss, then lead him to the bathroom before he could start.

Going to church helped with my stress… most of the time. One time, I came home from church planning to go out afterwards as a family. The kids weren't dressed and the house was a complete mess. I just lost it.

"Why can't you help out around the house?" I screamed at him. "Do you think I can do everything on my own? What's the matter with you?"

In response, Carlin stormed into our room and came back out with all of my clothes. He walked over to the door and threw them outside! "Get the fuck out of this house," he said, "so we can live in peace!" He turned to Anton and Sarah, who were still small, afraid and confused. "Kids, go get some of your mummy's clothes and throw them out, too. She's leaving." They hesitated, looked at me, but they too went into my room and took my things.

I didn't know what to do. I needed some help. The idea struck me: Mother had gone through this with her siblings and I thought she could help her own daughter. After speaking with her and explaining the situation she said she should come and talk some sense into him. I had no idea what to do.

Forty-five minutes later, the phone rang. "Fatima," said Mother. "I'm not coming over."

Her words stunned me into silence. "This is a matter between you and your man. I don't want to get involved. You're a grown woman. You can figure it out yourself."

A couple of seconds passed before I manage to say okay and hung up the phone.

She said nothing. Just clicked off the phone.

I hated her, oh how I hated her! In the months and years afterward I would not forgive her.

In the end, I had to call Carlin's mother, aunt and brother to come and get him. Unlike my own mother, they showed up. By the time they got there he was gone. His brother picked up my clothes and took them back in the house. "We'll talk to him," he said of Carlin. Afterwards, I never found out what they'd said. To this day, I can't quite remember how we got over that incident. The next day, we just went on as if nothing had happened.

But things would only get worse, and by "worse," I mean they got physical.

Another time, after the clothes incident, we were supposed to go to one of his family's barbecues. I wasn't keen on going. His daughter's mother was going to be there. For the life of me I couldn't understand why she had to come to every family event. I sat at home waiting for hours for him to come back. When he did, he was drunk and high.

"Seriously?" I said to him. "You know what? To hell with this barbecue. I'm going to take Sarah and we're going to get something else to eat."

"Fine," he said, "I'll take Anton and we'll go to the barbecue."

Hours later, we got home before they did. We walked through the doorway and I closed the door behind me and locked it, not thinking anything of it. I went and changed my clothes to relax for the evening.

Not long after that, someone knocked on the door, very hard. I walked down the hall and opened it. Carlin and Anton were there.

"What happened? You lose your keys?"

Carlin said nothing, but he had this swell-up look on his face. Anton took off his shoes and went to his room to go to sleep. I closed the door behind Carlin.

The next thing I knew, his hands were on my throat. I tried to scream out, but Carlin was squeezing too hard.

"Are you hiding the keys from me? What? You don't want me in this house? This is MY house!"

I had no idea what he was talking about, but I couldn't answer. Carlin pushed me against the kitchen counter and then let me go. I coughed, and as soon as I could talk, I stood up to him. "No man has ever laid hands on me! Not my father, no one!"

"Well, they should have!" he yelled back, "and it's going to start with me knocking your teeth down your throat!"

He grabbed my arms and tried again, but I fought back as best I could, standing my ground. My only consolation in that moment was that the balcony door was open. If things got out of hand, I could run out and call for help.

Huh, out of hand? Things had already gotten out of hand, but I couldn't see it!

As with our other fights, it burned itself out, but this time, I was officially in survival mode.

***

I withdrew into myself and my affections for him. Our special time on Sunday no longer happened and Carlin was hardly home on weekends, going out with God only knew who. No longer did I pick up after him nor did I do his laundry. Nope. I just went to work and came home like a robot.

The violence continued to interrupt the routine. One morning, while getting ready for work we had it out again. He forced me to pick up the dirty dishes and pushed me into the side table, breaking the lamp. I fought back with the comb I had in my hand, swiping it across his face, causing it to bleed.

He stormed out to the car, and when he saw just how much I had made him bleed, he called me up. "You are going to be sorry for making me bleed." I was so upset at work that my boss sent me home.

When I got back, I called his mother. "You need to talk to your son," I told her. "I'm not sure what his issue is, but he needs to keep his hands off me. I don't know if it's chemicals at work or whatever he's smoking, but he needs to stop."

She agreed to talk to him, and for the next two weeks, she would call everyday to see how things were going.

Somehow, I got over that wall, as I had all of the other walls I had met in my past, but I still had the idea of leaving in the back of my head. The bigger wall, that of my relationship as a whole with Carlin, was right in front of me, and there seemed to be no way over it. I had lost interest in him. Where there was once love, there was now only the need to get away from him. All my love would be saved for my children and only my children, never for another man.

Still, I remained blind to seeing all of this as the irrefutable sign I had prayed to get. As such, I remained where I was.

***

Five years after we moved into the condo, I decided that we should look for a house. The place was too small for our growing family. Carlin agreed, and we called the original agent to put the condo on the market. We cleaned everything up, and we started bidding on other places. This, I felt, could be an opportunity for me to leave.

I decided to open up to Mother about the idea of leaving. "Take control over every aspect of the new house," she said, "and don't let him contribute. You make all the decisions ahead of time and then make it seem like it was his choice."

"How do you know it'll work?" I asked her.

She simply replied, "That's what worked for me. Buy the house and stay in the relationship for another five years. That way, when you sell the house, you'll get more money out of the deal."

Sometimes, I really wondered what was going on in her head, but as sound as her thought process was, my priority wasn't about making more money, it was having peace of mind. That was worth more to me than more money from five more years of this crap.

Before long we'd found a beautiful house in Alliston, just gorgeous! Five bedrooms, three baths, on eleven acres of land for $245,000. Surely this place, far removed from the grind and grime of the Toronto suburban sprawl would be a great place to start over. We put in an offer but our condo wasn't selling. In the end, someone else beat us to the five bedroom home in Alliston.

Around the same time, Carlin's three year old niece was struck and killed by a speeding car. We were all heartbroken. I was really close with the girl's mom, as we were both pregnant at the same time. The relationship really went downhill from there. Carlin's family, for whatever reason, resumed picking on me and putting me down whenever we'd go over for visits. He never stood up for me.

When I was on good terms with Carlin's mom, I'd call her once in awhile, just to chat. On this particular occasion, she said, "my brother's going to St. Vincent on Wednesday for a wedding." I thought at the time ,"oh, how nice!" That was when a little voice from somewhere other than inside my mind said, "don't say anything to Carlin."

This was strange. Normally, anytime there was something going on with his own family, I'd share it. But I decided to follow that gut feeling and hold back.

Friday came around and Carlin came to the front door all dressed up in nice clothes. "Okay, honey, I'm going to play dominoes with my brother at my uncle's house." I looked at him and thought "Really? That's funny, your uncle's in St. Vincent." Still, I said nothing. He came over, kissed me and headed out the door. It was 8 o'clock.

At 10 o'clock, following my hunch, I called his cell phone. No answer. From that point on, I'd call him on the hour every hour throughout the night. I called his mother to ask where he was. She said she hadn't seen him. I called the brother he was supposedly playing dominoes with. "No," he said, "I have no idea where he is."

Finally, at 7 a.m., my phone rang. It was Carlin.

"Hey Fatima, what's up?'

"Where were you?" I asked. "You didn't come home and you weren't answering your phone."

"Oh, I'm on my way home now."

When he came back, Carlin sat on the couch and I sat across from him.

"So what happened? Where were you?'

"I went by my mother's house to hang out with Stan and then Derek came by and we hung out for a bit."

"What happened to going to your uncle's house?

"We did not end up going there."

"I know," I replied, "because your mother told me during the week he went home for a wedding.

Carlin could only say. "Oh… you should have told me."

"I called your mother's house and Stan said you were there and then you left. I actually called twice and your daughter told me you were there and then you left again."

Carlin seemed to shrink. "Oh… well, Derek borrowed my phone and left with it. That's why I didn't answer."

"So why did Derek not answer the phone?"

Carlin was stumped now. "Ummm….."

Another woman. I knew. I just knew.

Fighting back tears and rage, I simply said to him, "I will never forgive you for what you have done to this family."

I had gotten the irrefutable sign that I had asked for. I was going to leave. The question now became, how?

Over The Wall

Chapter Ten

My life has been a product of all the choices I made. My circumstances did not make up who I am, they were an opportunity for my true self to be revealed. I believe everything is in divine order: God, the universe, a higher power or whatever else people believe is in charge of it all. The knowing of something that is greater than ourselves provides solace. Guilt was a waste of mental energy and I needed to give that up. There was no point in me feeling guilty anymore as I could not save the relationship and I wanted to protect my kids from growing up with a single mom. I was that child and I couldn't bare to put my children through any of that. I dreamed of having a family and one that did not look like the one I grew up in. But now, I needed to save myself. It was clear that we both became addicted to the chaos and I was now handing over this addiction to God.

When I was going through my post-partum depression, I saw my mother in me. I was disgusted by what I heard ripple off my sharp tongue, the look of my face when I was nasty and how bitter I felt inside. It was at this time that I had a glimpse of why she was the way she was. She survived life. Her life was a day to day game; a constant fight with her circumstances, a fight with her moral conscience, and most of all, the constant internal battle of regret, every time she looked at me. Perhaps she was scared. Her relationships with men were not filled with love or at least not the kind of love that comes from healthy relationships. She grew up with no guidance; her father had cheated on her mother, and that was her understanding of relationships. For her, the men in her life may have been the best she was going to get and that worked for her. She may have built her own walls so that nothing could get in or out. Even when it seemed like she was happy with Clyde, it seemed she became numb and blind to how she was being treated. There was no way in hell I was going down that path. This generational curse, which dominated the minds of women to lower themselves and allow a man to degrade who they were and belittle their greatness, was not who I would be. More than anything else, it was not something I would allow my children to see. If I stayed, I would only be teaching them that it was ok to give permission to another person to treat you unjustly. I may not have had a lot of money and I may not have been able to give my kids the riches of materialistic possessions, but what I did have was the wealth of wisdom, knowing what was not right, and knowing I had the power to get us over that wall, keep running, and never look back.

My escape plan came together quickly.

By this time I was not interested in being intimate with Carlin anymore. Sex just became as robotic as the rest of my life. I had the entire process down to three minutes of my time that I would never get back. There were no other displays of affection like hugging or kissing. His mouth was like an ashtray and I wasn't interested in him at all. Sometimes, I wished he would never come home and it would just be me and the kids.

I decided to encourage Carlin to put the place back up for sale so we could go look for another house. The hope was that this would buy me some more time, but as it turned out, the first person who came to see our condo ended up buying it. My share of the sale amounted to about $25,000. Still, it put pressure on me to figure out the next step of the plan: where was I going to go?

One night, when I was just fed up with everything, I went to him in the livingroom. He was sitting in his chair, watching the NBA playoffs and drinking as usual.

"Carlin," I said, "I want the lawyer to give us two cheques for the house."

He didn't look away. "Why?" he asked.

"Because I want to move out on my own."

Carlin didn't move, didn't even look at me, didn't even shrug. "Fine," he said, "do what makes you happy."

I stayed quiet for a moment before continuing. "All right, I'll go live with my mother until I find another place."

He said nothing and went on watching his game. I knew, in my head, that he would never go to my mother's house because he couldn't smoke and drink there. Instead, he'd be forced to move in with his own mother.

I walked away to the bedroom and just lay there, staring at the ceiling, my head swimming with thoughts.

Twenty minutes later, Carlin stumbled in. "Let's have sex," he said.

I sat up. "Did you hear what I said before? I'm leaving and living on my own."

"Yes," he said. What a disaster this guy was! I walked out of the room, and Carlin, disappointed, collapsed onto the bed behind me.

***

I got my cousin Peggy involved in my plan. She was very supportive of me and she became a big reality check. In fact, she helped me see one thing that was in my blind spot for almost the whole relationship with Carlin, an obvious thing about him that I hadn't wanted to admit.

One morning, not long after the sale, we were at the gym together, doing warm-up stretches on the mats before getting on the treadmills.

"Seriously, Fatima," said Peggy, "do you realize that Carlin's an alcoholic?"

"That's nonsense," I replied. "He just drinks a lot. He's been doing that since we were teenagers."

"Uh huh, so you think that drinking at five in the morning is something that everyone does, right?"

I let that sink in for a moment while I stood up to stretch my arms.

"Yeah," I said finally, "I can see that, but he's a functional alcoholic."

The look on Peggy's face was mutinous, like she was gonna slap me right there in the gym. "Fatima, don't bullshit yourself. An alcoholic is an alcoholic. You carry that big box of empty bottles out of the house and you say that's normal? Just because he's not pissing himself walking out the door to go to work, you say he's "functional"? No, an addict's an addict. There's no such definition as 'functional.'"

I stood up and did some calf stretches. "I don't know about moving back in with my Mother."

"Why not?" said Peggy, "It's the obvious choice."

"Well, you know how she is. I know she has her judgments about my relationship with Carlin, but we never talk about it."

"If you never talk about it," said Peggy, reaching her arm back over her shoulder, "then how can you know that she has judgments?"

I turned and looked at her square in the eye. "Please, this is my Mother we're talking about, Peg. She and your mother have never had anything good to say about him. And do you remember the time when Carlin and I got into a fight and he threw all of my clothes out into the hallway?"

"I do."

"I called Mother to help with the kids. An hour later, she calls me back. Tells me 'I'm not coming anymore. I decided I don't want to get involved'."

Peggy sighed. "I remember. I get it. Look, this arrangement isn't forever. Plus, it'll give you extra time to find a place of your own. Plus, think of all the rent you could have for a down payment on another house of your own." I didn't say anything further as I knew she had a good point.

Once the ink was dry on the sale of the house, I stopped looking at houses with Carlin. I told him I was going to move in with my mother until I found another place to live. I don't think he quite got that I was leaving.

***

On my way to meet Peggy, at the gym one night, I called my mother from the car to talk about the moving arrangements.

"Sorry," said Mother out of nowhere, "I'm getting a beep. Let me take this."

I heard some buttons being pushed, then some new voice appeared on the line. It was Clyde. What the hell?

Mother had meant to put me on hold. I'm not sure what she did, but I heard her speak words that weren't intended for me to hear.

"I don't know why I have to listen to this shit all the time. I don't know why she bothers me with her stupid problems. She never should have been with him in the first place. Now I have to listen to her and her foolishness all the time." When she was finished her rant, and came back on the phone, I told her simply, "I heard all of what you said."

This time, I just bawled. There weren't enough words I could use to communicate the hurt I had just felt from my own mother, so I let my crying do the talking. To my surprise, Mother started to backpedal.

"Fatima, shh… it's alright."

"It's not alright!" I shouted back, "I heard everything you just said!"

"Oh…" That was all she said. No apology. No expression of regret. Just "oh."

I composed myself and spoke very deliberately. "Mother, I'm not moving in with you. I was going to ask you, but now instead, I will find an apartment and take the kids, and we will live on our own. We will get through this without your help because you don't really mean it. You've never supported my relationship with him and now you're not supporting me ending it. You want me to prove that I don't need your help? Congratulations, you've done it. Bye."

I hung up the phone and kept crying in the car. My insides burned with hatred, hurt and embarrassment at being so vulnerable with this woman who had never let me lower my guard for the entire time we'd known each other. And there was relief: the relief of years of having finally releasing words I'd wanted to tell her for a long, long, time.

When I was calm enough, I called Peggy to tell her what happened.

"All right, girl," she said, when I had finished, "let's find you a place."

"I… I can't take living one more moment than I have to with this man. I want us out."

"Don't worry," said Peggy, "I have an idea about that, too."

In June, I found a place that worked: a two bedroom apartment that was far enough away from our old home, but close enough to coordinate school for the kids and my work commute. I'd be able to move in, in July. I hadn't shared with Carlin what had happened between Mother and I.

For the next few weeks, I quietly packed up our things. Carlin would see the boxes, but didn't ask anything, assuming that it was part of me moving into my mom's place.

Finally, one night, everything was packed up. Carlin and I spent the night sleeping in the same bed. I lay awake, scared and nervous, thinking about the man beside me. Is this what men were, what they became? My father had been gone a long while, and my mother, raised in a culture that valued submissive women, had suffered, even if she never showed it. Was that now to be my fate? After I left, what would happen? How would I live as a single mother?

The kids: I decided that Anton and Sarah were my priority. I'd work, make money and take care of them to make sure they grew up right. Even though she had flaws, even though she herself didn't believe it at times, that's what my mother had done for me. I would do the same for them.

The next morning, Carlin woke me up with his usual nuzzling of my neck. I indulged his urges, and when it was over, I got up and showered. "I'm going to work," he called out from the bedroom. "Goodbye!"

"Bye!" I called back. He was gone. Time to move.

The truck showed up about 10 a.m., as did Peggy. The crew packed everything away into the truck. I had to let the kids in on this part of the plan. I couldn't tell them the whole truth, not just yet, though I'm sure Anton being the oldest, had figured out on some level just what we were doing.

Within two hours, everything that belonged to me had been packed into the truck. I left Carlin his couch, the kitchen table, most of the dishes and cutlery, and the TV. I walked around that empty house, feeling nervous in my stomach.

Peggy walked up from behind and put her hand on my shoulder. "Is that it.'

"It is… I dunno, am I really doing this? Is this really happening?"

"Yes," replied Peggy. "Fatima, this is your freedom. This is the day you're done with this relationship. It's a new start."

I listened to how our voices echoed in the mostly empty house. "How many new starts am I going to have before I'm over the wall?" I asked.

Peggy didn't answer. She just smiled and led me outside. I stood in that front hallway one last time, the place where Carlin had shoved me when I was pregnant and I remembered so many other petty acts of violence, now at an end. Carlin would come back to the empty house that he had helped to create. But for all of what had happened, I didn't hate the man. I saw he needed help, and I also had to do right by my kids, to protect and nurture the family that we had started.

I said a silent goodbye to that hallway, and to that house, then walked out the door for the last time.

As I followed the truck to the new house, I hit 'scan' on the FM radio in my car. It stopped at the Buffalo station. "It's July 4th," the announcer said, "Happy Independence Day!"

***

Carlin didn't call for two days. We had settled in by then and I decided to call him.

"You couldn't have called me sooner?" he said quietly. I could hear hurt, anger and sadness in his voice. My reflexes shot up before I remembered: he can't touch you here. He can't hurt you over the phone.

"I did what I had to do," I replied.

"Let me come over and see the kids."

"No," I said. "Just give us a few days. Let us settle in first."

Carlin said nothing for a few seconds, then "alright, a few days."

He hung up.

Within the week, Carlin called. And then again. Every day, he would call, ask to speak to the kids, and say the same thing. "Tell your mom that you want to see me and I want to come over." The kids would speak with him and then they would beg to see their father. Why wouldn't they? How do you tell your children they can't see their dad? How can you do that?

Finally, I'd had enough. "Carlin," I said, "you need to stop manipulating the kids like this. I have no intention of keeping you from them, but I know how you get. That's why we're here!"

The visits started and went mostly without incident. Carlin convinced me to go for counseling. We weren't married, so it wasn't court mandated or anything. We only ended up going to two sessions. He spent Christmas with us. He would come over and bathe the kids and bring them dinner.

Carlin hadn't stopped drinking. That's not how addiction works. He never stopped during all of this time.

By January of 2005, we'd gotten ourselves into a stable pattern. Then, one day when he was leaving to go home, Carlin dropped a bombshell.

"So, when do I get the key?"

"Um… you don't."

Carlin blinked. "What the hell are you saying? I come over every other goddamn day to see my kids and I don't get a key?"

"We're not getting back together Carlin. You can come visit, but you're not living here."

The look he gave me was deadly. "All right… you still have some of my things from before. When can I pick them up?"

I was afraid of that look, but I held my ground. "Okay. I will let you know." It was a couple of weeks before he came to get his stuff.

When he did pulled up in his Jeep, I could tell he was very angry. I did not want to get into anything with him because the kids, my cousin and her children were also at my house. He stormed past me and went inside to get his things. As he started to move his things out of the house, he seemed to get angrier and angrier, which got my back up as I watched him.

Then, everything exploded.

"Get off the rug!" he shouted at the kids. They were standing on the rug he was going to take with him.

"Don't yell at them like that!" I said back.

Before I knew it, Carlin had grabbed me by the throat, thrown me up against the wall, and pulled back his fist as if to punch me. Sarah screamed. Toni picked up the phone.

"I'm gonna call the police Carlin!" she said. He looked at her, then back at me. He let me go, grabbed the last of his things and packed them into the Pathfinder. As he pulled away, Toni called the police anyway.

Two officers arrived not long after that. I couldn't believe this was happening to me! This was the second time the cops had come. We explained what happened, and as we did, one of them frowned at me. "You have a scratch on your face ma'am," he said. I put my hand on it. It was bleeding. I treated the cut and the police took notes for a report.

"We don't need your consent," said the officer in charge, "we're going to file charges and issue a warrant for his arrest." I concurred. This was the last time I would hit the wall with Carlin and this time, there would be no turning back.

Ultimately, Carlin turned himself into the police and we ended up going to court. Because Anton and Sarah were involved, I had to sit down with a social worker from The Children's Aid Society to reassure them the kids were in good care.

For the next several months, I couldn't sleep right. I would hear every single noise outside the apartment and get up to check it out. In the dead of night, I would get up from my bed and pace to the front door, back and forth, worried that Carlin was lurking just outside.

The kids, too, felt the impact of their dad's behaviour, long after he was gone. One night, someone was lighting up a joint somewhere down the hall. Anton said to me.

"Hey Mummy," he said, "do you smell that?"

"I do," I said to him.

"It reminds me of daddy."

At that moment, I knew I had done the right thing for my children. They were not going to grow up knowing weed the same way other kids knew the smell of cologne. They would never grow up believing that having their father beating up their mother was normal.

When the court date arrived, Peggy came with me. During the proceedings, we found out Carlin had another charge logged against him, on the books, for hitting another woman. Ultimately, the justice let him go, warning him that if he ever did it again, it would be his third strike and he would go to jail.

The judge issued a peace bond, which is a restraining order against him for one year that stopped him from seeing the kids on a regular basis. I was then able to change my phone number and get it legally blocked so that he would never be able to call me directly. Carlin was still allowed to call my cell to speak to the kids, though.

I decided that men were only good for "exercise," and there was otherwise no point in keeping them around. They would never get close to my children and they would never hurt them.

***

Carlin had visitation rights. I would take them to my mother's and he met them there. The arrangement was hard on us all, but I needed my sanity and to not sleep with one eye open.

I started working out, spending money on myself; slowly putting my life back together. What I did not do was to tell the children the truth about the separation. We had both told them that this would be a temporary thing. I felt that they were too young to understand, at three and five years old, the whole truth of it right now. I would explain it when they got older. Plus, it wasn't like they never saw their father.

Carlin still didn't accept that it was over between he and I. The journey into single motherhood was never my plan and I resented it at times. Still, I pressed on and did the best I could with help from my mother, sister and cousins. I had to put a lot aside for the sake of the children.

I still had my part of the $25,000 that we got from the condo sale. I had saved it for a down payment on a house and so I went looking. This time, I wasn't going to settle for just any house: I wanted the house. That search took me to a city I had never lived in before: Brampton, which is just northwest of Toronto.

There, I found a beautiful five-level townhome that seemed like an absolute palace that was within my price range! It was also a freehold, meaning that a condo board didn't own it, so I didn't have any condo fees. It had a garage that I could just drive into during the winter months, never having to feel the cold! It even had a pink room for Sarah and a blue room for Anton. Perfect! I made an offer and got it!

That summer, I told the kids we were moving. By that time, it had been a while since the incident with Mother over the phone. We had been cordial with each other, and the kids still spent the summer at her house, so cutting her out completely had never been an option. I had the freedom to work decorating the new place. By the time we brought them to see the new place everything was set up for the kids: beds, desks, dressers, everything.

When it was done, my sister, Mother, Clyde and Ma brought the kids over. The reaction on their faces was priceless and something I'll never forget! They were so excited to enjoy their rooms without worrying about unpacking. It was like they had instantly gotten a new start.

For me, though, the joy was short lived. As night fell, I got up from my bed, after trying in vain to fall asleep, and paced the house in the dead of night. Would Carlin find out where we were? Would he just show up? Would he call and ruin everything? Whenever there's a case of domestic abuse or addiction, Child Services gets called to determine if you're fit as a parent. They delved into the details of my life, scrutinized everything. I felt like the criminal, not Carlin. In the end, they did see I was fit to have custody, but that experience had left me shaken.

If Carlin were to come back again, and I was forced to call the police once more, would he ruin everything? The next three years were hell.

***

One of my favorite quotes is by Agatha Christie, "A mother's love for her child is like nothing else in the world. It knows no law, no pity, it dares all things and crushes down remorselessly all that stands in its path." When I think of my own mother I feel a void, as this was never my experience. But one thing is for certain, the woman I am today, the pain and rejection I have experienced, caused me to become the type of mother who will put her life on the line for her children. That generational curse that bounded mothers before me to survive motherhood stopped with me. My children's happiness was my happiness and their pain became my pain.

The children had had their fair share of witnessing the fights between Carlin and I. Between the yelling, the crying, slamming of doors, the physical violence, and his drinking, the space they lived in was not a space for two young children. This is what pained me the most. I saw myself in them. Isolated, their self-expression suppressed, and instead of being able to experience family love, they were in a constant horror movie of family pain.

This broke my heart. In addition, the death of their cousin hurt them. I cannot stress enough how much a child develops in the first 10 years of their life. They become who they are in life as a result of their environment and it is the most important time of their development. It is when the blueprint gets created that it will guide them the rest of their lives. Here I was, comforting them through their heart ache over their deceased cousin, trying to protect them from what was happening between their father and I, and all at the same time, struggling emotionally to keep my shit together by remaining strong and focused. I could handle the strife of my relationship, but I do not think anything could have prepared me for what was coming next.

"Mommy, I want to kill myself," said Anton.

"I want to go with him," said Sarah.

Words of horror that no mother ever wants to hear. The devil came and stabbed my heart with a burning sword straight out of hell. This wasn't happening and yet, yes it was!

It was clear that what was happening between Carlin and I was impacting the children way beyond anything I ever imagined. Anton was only 6 and Sarah 4. Too young to be bearing this kind of burden on their souls. Dear God, how have you forsaken me? Where are you? Pain me, do what needs to be done on MY life, but please, please, please spare my children. Dropping to my knees I was begging the Lord to have mercy on me. I was desperate for God's mercy.

I found the strength through faith. My head became clearer and I knew what I needed to do. I right away took the children to a therapist. This was a wall. I would say the hardest and tallest wall I would ever have to face, but I WOULD get over it.

When I took them to the therapist, she advised me that the children wanted to tell their father what they had shared with me about killing themselves. I feared another ugly scene, but this needed to be dealt with. I phoned Carlin and advised him to meet us at the local Wendy's, where we would be waiting for him.

When Carlin walked in, I was beside myself with anxiety. He sat down opposite us looking around at the busy patrons before focusing on us.

"So," he said to Anton and Sarah, "what do you want to tell me?"

Anton, ever the big brother, started first. "Daddy," he said, "we want to kill ourselves."

The words seemed to slap Carlin across the face. Part of me watched it and felt "damn right, you bastard! You deserve to feel that!" but mostly, I was sad for my children. Inside, my heart broke, and I did my best not to show it. "If I died," continued Anton, "then we would go to heaven."

"I want to die too," said Sarah in her quiet, sweet little voice. "So I can be with Anton in Heaven."

"How are you both going to do that?" I asked them.

"We'll run in front of a car and let it hit us, just like our cousin."

As the kids spoke, I had hoped that Carlin would find some kind of compassion, that I could look to him for emotional support. Instead, Carlin got up and walked out. Both Anton and Sarah started to cry and wail and I was left to tend to two very upset little kids. I was heartbroken and furious all at once. What the hell, to hear those words, see his children bear their souls, and then walk away when it was too hard to deal with!

I put the kids in the car and went back to my mother's. Carlin showed up twenty minutes later, not threatening, but simply to talk. "I'm sorry I left," he said. By then, I was too disappointed to say anything. He just could not take what they were saying.

I reported back to the therapist and the conclusion was that they wanted to be with their cousin. They were grieving her death, as young as they were, because it had an impact on them, especially my son, who was the same age.

Carlin's vindictiveness grew. He deposited a blank envelope in the bank, which caused my mortgage check to bounce. When I took him to court for child support, he claimed he made considerably less per year than when we'd lived together, which reduced his support payments by a third. He kept those payments up for two years before stopping completely. He didn't send us another payment of support for three years, and when he started back up, he was only paying $22 per month, for two children.

During those times, my little voice kept talking to me. "Turn it over to God," it said, "and watch it transform in front of you."

I wanted peace for my family, but there was no way of avoiding dealing with Carlin. He was the kids' father after all. Unfortunately that also meant that we couldn't always have peace. When the phone calls resumed for normal things like visiting the kids at Christmas and on birthdays, the conversations were okay for the most part, but some old patterns don't change without something massive happening.

Fortunately, I underestimated my son. About a year and a half into the new house when Carlin and I were on the phone. It was late at night on a Tuesday and Carlin was making his usual demands to get more than what I was ready to give.

"Listen, Carlin," I said, "you need to ask yourself: are you contributing to the children spiritually, physically, mentally, and financially?"

"No," he said.

"Then why should we have anything else to do with you outside the basics?"

Carlin started to shout into the phone. I lost my shit and shouted back. After about a minute of this, I heard a noise coming down the stairs to the kitchen. Anton came walking over to me in his pajamas, rubbing his eyes. "Mom, who are you talking to?" he asked.

"Your dad," I said.

Anton sighed. "Give me the phone for a second?"

I handed the receiver to him. "Daddy… it's Anton. Look, you're upsetting Mommy, she's yelling and screaming, and I can't sleep. You have to get off the phone now."

Anton clicked the "end" button and handed me back the receiver. Without a word, he walked back upstairs to bed, leaving me stunned. Look at my son go!

The next morning, I saw the phone ring. It was Carlin again. I girded up my loins for another fight when suddenly, I heard a small voice, seemingly from inside me.

Say to him, "I rebuke you in the name of Jesus Christ."

What the hell?

I didn't want to say that! I let the phone ring out, only to have him call back ten seconds later.

Say to him, "I rebuke you in the name of Jesus Christ."

I picked up the phone. Carlin started up.

"Who do you think you are, you dumb-"

"I rebuke you in the name of Jesus Christ!"

Carlin stopped. Then, he said something that made no sense. "Oh, I didn't sleep with her."

Neither of us spoke for a moment. What did he say?

"I never said you slept with anybody," I said finally, "what are you talking about?"

Silence. Then, he hung up the phone. Carlin didn't call back for a long time. Even though I had a lot of unanswered questions about whoever this person was he "didn't" sleep with, all I cared about was that maybe now, finally, we could have peace in our new house.

With my self worth being at its lowest, I knew there was no such thing as living a pain free life. There is evil and there is God. God does not create our pain, as it is us, here on earth, who cause it. Yet, I believe God is there to heal us if we will allow it. I handed myself and my children over to God's love. I knew I may not have all the answers and that I was guilty of contributing towards the situation we were in. I also knew that I was handing my future over to my faith and with that, I would get over the wall.

GETTIN MY GROOVE BACK

Chapter Eleven

The older we get, the harder we have to fight to create a new identity for ourselves. One that doesn't remind us of our past and empowers us to live our life on our own terms. There I was, a single mother of two, depressed, frumpy, with a wardrobe consisting of little more than sweat pants, bras that had my tits hanging like tube socks and granny panties. What happened to me? As I stood in front of the mirror, I no longer recognized the person I had become as me. But I did recognize her. There she was, Mother staring right back at me, through my own eyes. Everything I was feeling: all my hurt, pain and the fear I felt was showing on my face. I had let myself go. I looked like my life: A WRECK!

I was once again single. One thing was for sure, I would never get married or live common law again. Life is easier when you're by yourself or was I just trying to convince myself? What I knew for sure was that before I could even consider moving in the direction of another relationship, I needed to get my shit together and start looking like a woman again. I may not be happy on the inside, but one thing I knew was that I'll fake it until I make it if I have to. I remember the day I woke up, wide eyed, went to the bathroom, looked in the mirror and said "this is it!" In that moment I made the decision to clean myself up and get back to feeling sexy.

First thing I did was buy new clothes: a new coat and lots of new lingerie. I love to wear matching bras and panties. I think it's sexy. As I went about my day, having them on underneath was my way of reminding myself I was not dead and my 'parts' still worked! I gave up the dark coloured crew neck shirts and started to show some skin. I no longer walked out of the house without jewelry, makeup, my hair done and of course my high heels. Nothing boosts a woman's confidence like a pair of sexy stilettos.

My hair started growing back. I gave up the wigs and extensions and went to a barber to create a hot short look, one that was mine, all mine. And... I looked amazing!

I was on my way. I was getting my groove back. I purchased a new home and a car. Don't get me wrong, buying a house is not an essential step in getting your groove back, but if you need one and you can afford it, it doesn't hurt, and it certainly worked for me. I was doing well, free and independent of the stress of Carlin and all of his family's bullshit. Life was looking up. Whenever I saw Carlin or any of his family members, I made sure the children and I looked amazing.

After spending some time getting back my groove, I started back on the dating scene. At this point in my life, men for me were for one thing only: "Gettin' me some." I would share my view with other women and they would say I sound like a man. But I just spent the last few years of life struggling, battling, and losing myself, so the last thing I needed was a man holding me down again. I had needs and just because I'm a woman, doesn't mean I can't be straight about it.

I could not blame anyone for how my life unfolded up until now. I often did not know what to say about it, but one thing was for sure, I needed the time to believe in myself.

Life was moving forward. I had taken on a new part-time opportunity with a network marketing company. I bought into the dream of financial independence and freedom. With that position, came out of town training and conferences, and so I visited Atlanta. I remember lying on my bed, eyes wide open staring at the ceiling, still getting used to the fact that I was in a hotel room, away on business, independent and free. It was time to get up and get ready for the conference.

I was in the bathroom looking at myself in the mirror and that is when it hit me. It's my birthday! Not any ordinary birthday either. I was turning 40. I took my nightie off and stood naked in front of the mirror. "Dear lord," I said. When did my boobs start to droop ? What is all this roundness on my belly and love handles? I could squeeze myself like a bean bag. Where did the time go? More importantly: where did my body go?

I heard the 40's are the best years of a woman's life. I wasn't too sure about that. But, I was also optimistic. I did not need a lot materialistically. What was important were my kids, our health and more than anything, happiness.

Anton and Sarah were growing up and doing well. I had a secure full time job working in IT and believe it or not, Mother and I started having a real relationship! Not sure what happened to change it all around. We never talked about why things were as they were, but right now it was good and I was soaking it all in.

The non-stop drama and arguments with Carlin were a fading memory, though not without the odd reminder. Just as I arrived in Atlanta, Carlin called me. He seemed adamant on going another round with me, but this time I asked him the same question I had asked before. "Are you willing to contribute to our lives, mine and the children's, financially, physically, emotionally and spiritually?"

"No," was his response.

"Then there is no need for further discussions. When you're able to do so, then call me. I'm not in the country currently and I don't have the time or energy for this conversation." Then, I just hung up the phone. It felt amazing!

After my shower I dried myself off, put my clothes on, and took my 40 year old body back to the mirror. The face staring back at me still didn't look a day over 35! Thank God for that at least, and I was happier than I had been in a long time. I was also grateful for that. I closed my eyes, and without any kind of forethought, the words came to me.

"Dear God," I said, "I know my life wasn't what I wanted it to be in my 30s. In my 40s, going forward, I do not want it to be more of the same. I want to live a life that is totally different. And I'm going to put you in it. I'm going to pray. I've heard your voice: you've gotten me out of situations before and I'm going to continue to serve you because that's what I need to do."

I opened my eyes. The woman in the mirror looked the same, but something felt different. I felt the Spirit of God surge through my veins. Something was lifted, hope came through and just like that, my doubts and fears shifted.

***

I returned home from Atlanta only to be heading back to the airport a few days later. Knowing my life experience with Mother, no one, especially me, would ever believe that we would be going on an all-inclusive vacation to Jamaica. The power of my prayer was already at work. Just like that, I was at the resort, with Mother, Anton, Sarah and believe it or not, Clyde. Who would have imagined? The thought did creep into my mind that perhaps this was their way of redeeming themselves. I stopped thinking and returned to being in bliss.

***

I was back at my desk like nothing had happened. My ass was in this chair as I stared at a computer screen, but my mind was still on the beach recalling the sound of the wind and the peace of paradise. I had not been able to stop thinking about God and our conversation. Yes I prayed, but that was not any ordinary prayer. That was a conversation with God. I knew He was there. I felt His presence in my spirit. Somewhere deep down inside I knew that life was going to change, but when? "Patience Fatima, patience," I told myself.

I was at my job for 5 years and it was like pulling teeth trying to to find avenues for growth and development. I couldn't even get out of my department, so I started looking for a new job. Atlanta, Jamaica and my conversation with God became a distant memory. For some reason, I was finding myself going downhill again. I was feeling tired all the time, slightly depressed, I had chronic constipation, heavy menstrual cycles and I couldn't stop eating foods that were full of sugar and salt. I would go to work, cook, clean, take care of the kids, watch TV and go to bed. And it would start all over again the next day.

What was happening to me? I was on such a good path! I picked myself up and now it seemed like I was on my way down again. I became scared and asked God to hear me.

One day, I was walking into the office and felt my stomach churning again. It was gas. I had had this problem for years. Do you know how hard it is to focus on work when you feel you need to fart all the time? God forbid it smells! Thank God there were so many men that worked around me as everyone would just blame them. A co-worker approached me because she could tell something wasn't right with me. She recommended I see a Traditional Chinese doctor named Antonella, who had helped her cousin. I called her and made an appointment.

I took the first appointment she had. I entered an office with beige overtones and chairs that were obviously arranged in a kind of feng shui pattern. Chinese letters hung on the walls. I wondered what she would look like? Was she a wise ancient Asian woman? I could only visualize what I saw in movies. The door opened and out came this fair skinned Italian woman. She said, "Hello" and I told her I was waiting for the doctor. Antonella said, "I'm Antonella" and shook my hand. "Come on in."

With Antonella's help, I discovered quite a few things that were not working with my health. For starters, I wasn't sleeping properly at all, getting up almost every night at 3 a.m. to go pee. I was averaging only about 5 hours worth of sleep and I was also dreaming quite a bit. "Dreaming stops you from going into deeper sleep," she told me, "leaving you tired the next day."

My sweet cravings were due to issues with my period. Whenever it came around, I'd have to wear two different sized bras because my breasts would swell and become tender. I'd also become very angry and irritable in the process.

"Eating all of those foods also has put a strain on your digestive system," Antonella continued. "It's not always the usual suspects when it comes to bad foods. Look for what gives you heartburn and bloating. There are specific things that you shouldn't eat based on your own body's physiology." Bad eating had also forced me to take laxatives so I could poop and that wasn't good, either.

All of this added up to a lack of energy, which explained why I would start to fall asleep on the job at 10 a.m. and 3 p.m., and why I just walked around with this awful feeling most of the time.

"Almost all of this starts with the stress you're under," said Antonella. "You're not being real with the stress levels that you're operating under."

I thought about it. The breakup with Carlin, the responsibilities of owning a home, working in a ridiculous environment, while raising two children on my own. I definitely had more than my fair share of stressors.

Well, I could not think of one thing that Antonella was wrong about. She was spot on. I made an appointment to come back the next week to pick up the herbs she prescribed for me and get a list of what was in them. She also recommended a cleanse in the new year. I was to take the herbal pills twice a day with plenty of water. I was also to start drinking four glasses of water, which had always been a struggle for me. I was instructed to do the strangest thing: I was to note information about my poop, such the colour, shape, how hard it was and if it had mucus.

But you know what? It did wonders! I started going to the washroom regularly, not every two days, which is what I thought was normal. I soon began to realize how much better I felt and I lost 10 lbs of poop! Go figure! What was really wrong with me was that I was full of shit!

During my cleanses, Antonella gave me a new list of foods to eat, foods to avoid and other actions I should take. Before long, the 'fall fog' started to lift. I started to feel so much better. My stomach stopped acting up. The anxiety went away with the acidity, and suddenly, I felt good! I mean, who ever really thinks about how good it feels to be in a their body?

My period came the next month without any of the PMS symptoms I had been suffering with for the last twenty years. I was loving this woman for this alone! She is a miracle worker! I started sleeping better and had more energy.

***

I was feeling great. A new me! I had not felt this healthy and alive for as long as I could remember. I started adding color to my wardrobe. I even began to listen to the Joyce Meyers CD's that my cousin had given me. I loved the messages and began to apply them to life.

For the next few weeks, life started to feel like it had taken on a new energy. I woke up feeling refreshed. My body was happy that I was feeding it things that were good for it. Then, not long after, something totally unexpected happened.

There was this guy at work. A white guy, about 45, named Kevin. Developer, divorced, raising his kids on his own. In almost all the right ways, Kevin had it going on! No pot belly, size 32 waist, quite fit.

I had to admit, having that bit of eye candy at work took the edge off the day, walking past him in the halls and in the kitchen. Mmm… stud muffin of the office! And one day, he turned to me. "Fatima," he said, as I was walking past.

"Oh, hi Kevin," I said. We'd never talked before. What could he want?

"Hey… um, I'm working on a project and need access to some network files. Can you grant me access?"

Kevin was looking at me, smiling from his eyes. Cute and friendly. I nodded. "Sure!" I said. He thanked me and stepped away.

The next time we talked was at the Christmas pot luck, which I was helping to organize. I don't remember exactly what he said, just that he was pretty slick, first by making friendly chit chat, and then by asking me how old I was.

Then one day, he emailed me: "Hey Fatima, listen, there's a great Thai restaurant that just opened up not far from here. Do you want to join me for lunch?"

I didn't know what to make of it, so I just replied "Sure! Where is it?"

He sent me the address and suggested we meet there, driving separately, "so as not to raise suspicion."

That day, I pulled up to the restaurant, wondering if he'd actually follow through on his intention. Sure enough, there he was, waiting at the door with a big grin on his face. He gave me a little wave. I waved back, but I was hesitant.

See, at eight years old I decided that white boys didn't like black girls because the year I moved to Canada I was teased for being too skinny, having big lips and teeth so white they could see them in the dark! And that decision was reinforced when that white boy spat in my face and called me "nigger." I decided from that day onward that white boys didn't like black girls. I also made it mean that they'd have even less reason to like me because back when I got to Canada, I was too skinny, I talked funny, my lips were too big and my teeth were so white you could see them in the dark!

So naturally, I was more than a bit suspicious about Kevin.

"What does he want?" I asked my cousin Peggy on the phone later that same day.

"I don't know," she said. "Maybe he's looking to take advantage of your vulnerable state."

"What do you mean?"

"You know, some men do that. They find a woman who's single, maybe's going through some kind of personal crisis, then they take advantage." She paused, then continued. "Who knows? Maybe he's married and looking to step out."

If that last one was the case, Kevin would not have been the first. Years ago; before Carlin, I was approached by a couple of married men who had a lot of sad stories about their wives.

One of them, let's call him "Stan," told me upfront "Yes, I am married, and I'm not leaving my wife. And no, I won't say bad things about her to you."

I asked him why he was calling me, if that was the case? He said, "Oh, because I like you, and I want to be with you."

"So why me? What's your motivation to ask me instead of someone else?"

"Well… you just seem so vulnerable, that's all."

I tried it out. Frankly, whatever was wrong in his marriage was between him and his wife. I wished I hadn't as the guy turned out to be too pushy, telling me that I was too materialistic, watching too much TV and not really offering much except for 'exercise.' I ended it as quickly as I could.

Not long after that first man, I had a second guy who told me straight up he was going to leave his wife. We ended up going to dinner. He was a good talker and seemed very charming, but I wasn't convinced I wanted to have anything to do with him. My gut feeling, it turns out, was right: not long after that, I had a woman calling me claiming to be his girlfriend, who had just had his son. A few months after that, a different woman phoned me up just to call me nasty names. I wasn't sure who she was, but I told her I wasn't involved with him. She didn't believe me. "Nope, I'm calling up the woman he lives" with she said. I said that was a good idea and to call me back to let me know how the call went. Now she's not too smart because she was calling his wife. A few days later, she called back to apologize, crying. Turns out this 'Prince Charming' not only had a wife, but two mistresses, and possibly a third.

This is what the single life brings, I thought. Maybe it was the wigs and the weaves that I wore. Maybe they just attract a certain type of man.

But was Kevin going to be any different? We started seeing each other frequently, not long after that first lunch, so whoever he was, I was going to find out soon enough.

***

Once again, it was "prep time!" Kevin earned a longer prep time. I prepared myself in a way that even turned me on. I do not think men really get how much work it takes for a woman to get ready for them, I mean who else are we doing it for? We have a lot at stake and the pressure is on. A guy has it easy: he can just get in the shower, maybe trim his beard a little, put on some cologne and a nice fitting shirt and pants, shiny shoes, and he's good to go. I drifted into my head wondering if he will do some 'manscaping.' Nothing worse than a man going "au natural," especially the hairy ones. For women, prep time can take anywhere from two hours to a whole day. You gotta make sure the bush is trimmed or for those that like it smooth and clean you need to take time making sure you did not give yourself a cut or two. Ouch, that's the worst! I heard stories of my guy friends saying sometimes they feel they are going for a feeding in the Amazon. Picking the right outfit is an art. That can take weeks! I won't even talk about shoes. Men need to know that by the time they show up to pick us up, we have put in the same number of work hours as a warehouse worker at Christmas, but with none of the payoff.

We went to a restaurant on the airport strip and had a good time. We danced and we drank and we went home. And that was that. It was my first good date in a long time.

There are men that become one of those milestones, the ones that teach us great things about ourselves. I believe Kevin came into my life for the purpose of building my self-confidence back up.

"I want you to change my look," I said to him during one of our lunch dates. "Can you help me with that?"

"Absolutely!" he said.

We went shopping and I was surprised to learn how much Kevin knew about women's fashion. We got clothes and bras to match my new look. I went from wearing a crew neck shirt to a v-neck, from wearing cloth bras to padded push-ups. Now, I was still very shy, so I would wear the v-necks with a sweater or jacket on top to keep myself covered.

On one of our dates, I was still wearing a jacket to cover up. Kevin said, "What's up with you? You're trying to get away from that." Kevin was really the first person to help me select the type of bras that were comfortable. How he knew so much about that, I had no idea!

Pretty soon, my date prep involved me wearing two inch stilettos, nylons and a hot, brightly-coloured dress that showed off some skin and my curves.

"You look good!" he kept saying, "and you've got a sexy body."

It was good to hear, but it was a challenging transition, one of the hardest I've ever done. Why wasn't I happy with my transformation? And why was I still holding back with Kevin?

I had been seeing a therapist to sort these issues out, but he was starting to piss me off, so I stopped going. Before I stopped, my therapist told me one way to get my self-esteem and energy back was to organize social events. That was good advice, so I started putting together everything from girls nights and game nights to a Canada Day weekend barbecue. And it worked! Life started to seem happy and juicy to me, thanks to the fun times I was having with my girlfriends.

I continued seeing Kevin, I also continued to take the time to prep, and I didn't mind at all. Here was a good man, a solid gentleman with integrity who seemed very interested in me. None of this married man crap! Throughout all of our time together, I created in my mind that I wanted someone who lived near me. No expensive long distance phone calls or long commutes across the gridlock to see each other. A man who had a car, a job and had a place to bring me home to because I was not going to introduce anyone to my children in my house. In fact, under no circumstances were they going to meet my children. I was not getting serious with anyone, Kevin included. No, they were only going to be good for exercise.

***

We dated almost 8 months, but no romance blossomed out of it. Kevin and I never argued, didn't have any problems per se, except that there was this threshold of closeness that we never quite crossed.

Nearly a year after Kevin asked me out, I found myself inside a party room listening to a happy-looking Filipino guy talk about a personal development program. We did this exercise in a workbook that helped us distinguish what areas of our life were important and what areas of our life were not working. I discovered something about myself that was missing and I wanted to know more. I was able to get a glimpse of what it would look like if I was confident and free from regret and resentment, so I registered!

A month later I found myself in a room with approximately 150 other people. We had an assignment to write a letter to someone in our life where we were holding back something from them. I choose to write to Kevin.

There, sitting up in bed in my mom's guest room just before midnight, yellow pad and pen in hand, I wrote the letter by the lamplight.

"Dear Kevin," I began. "I don't like the way my life is going. You and I have been having a lot of fun, but it's just mechanical, going through the motions, and I want more out of a relationship. I want to be a in a relationship with somebody. I don't know if that's you, but that's where my life is headed."

After the seminar was finished, I went back to work on Monday, tired, but buzzing with waves of transformative energy. I brought the letter with me and read it to Kevin.

"Wow!" he said, looking it over. "I'm... really flattered that you chose to be this honest with me."

"Well, of course. You deserve to know that I care about you, I really do."

Kevin seemed hesitant. The smile on his face was solid, like it was painted alfresco on clay. "Thank you! That'll definitely give us something to talk about over drinks." He folded the letter, leaned over and kissed me. "I'll call you before Saturday to set it up?"

I smiled. "Sure thing."

"Great!" Kevin walked over to his desk and I walked over to mine.

He never called. We stayed office friends and he went back to being Office Kevin, and that was that. In that moment a miracle happened, I was okay. I didn't make the situation wrong. I did not go into my head and say I was not good enough. I simply accepted his choice and that was that. Instead, I was grateful for our experience together as he was a very important part of my growth, feeling sexy and expanding myself sexually. That program allowed me to see what I really wanted for my life; that I was pretending I did not want love, and that I didn't want to be with a man. It had me see I was lying to myself. I was able to forgive and let go of a lot. Most of all I knew this was a turning point. Something big was going to happen and best of all it was because now I knew I had the power this whole time to create any possibility for my life that I wanted and I could have it anytime.

My Search For Butterflies

Chapter Twelve

I do not know where I am going, but I will meet you there. I close my eyes and there he is. The man I believe in and who believes in me. Our bodies merging into one another and naturally fitting, designed to be one. I remember you in my possibility. I created you in my thoughts and my faith will bring you to me.

How can love be so addictive and at the same time carry so much pain? I cannot blame the men who could not make me happy or give me what I needed. I barely knew what I wanted myself let alone who I was. We often look at wanting things to be better, as if what we have, and where we are now is not good. It's only when we can look back, as we stand in our bliss, that we see why our life had to unfold as it did.

After Kevin and my transformational program, I started peeling away the past. I was discovering what it felt like for the first time to really forgive: Myself, Mother, Father and Carlin. I let go of years of pain. I began to set myself free and most of all, allow faith to touch my spirit reaching through that wall of hate.

I decided to take a timeout from dating and socializing and focused on "me."

I continuously listened to motivational speakers and people of faith with inspiring messages of hope.

The program I took forever changed me, lifting from me years of pain, and giving me a new perspective on life. I was becoming someone I did not even recognize. I even started to accept Carlin for who he was and who he was not. I began to see what I wanted to commit my life to. I was clear that true forgiveness is giving up the hope that the past could have been different. I was seeing life through a new set of eyes and it felt so free.

With this new sense of self, I also began to create new relationships by simply giving people a chance. I gave up judging them and making them wrong for everything. I created the possibility of love, and being in love, and as scary as it was, I said out loud, "I want to get married." I knew that was going to take a lot more work on my part but I said it anyway!

One day I came across some old journals from high school. Among them, there were entries about my mother, Carlin… and Ronald Gould. Wow! How long had it been since I had seen him? I turned the page to April 7th and remembered that that was Ron's birthday.

Ronald Gould. Someway, somehow he never left my thoughts. How is it that just standing up for me and that one kiss could stay with me for this long. He was like a tattoo on my heart. Most girls see losing their virginity as a moment that forever stays with them. For me, with all the men I had kissed in my life, Ron was the one who left his imprint on my lips, on my heart, and on my soul.

***

One day I was introduced to this movie called "The Secret." I could not believe what I was hearing. The law of attraction, shifting your universe, what you think about and what you bring about. WOW! It was so in-line with what I had discovered in that program that we create our world with our words and our words all come from our thoughts. This made so much sense to me. Everything was happening so fast. My thoughts were changing. Every day I was consumed with wanting to be a greater person. I was hungry for more. I watched 'The Secret' so many times that my kids ended up knowing this movie by heart.

When Joyce Meyers came to Toronto that year, I volunteered at her event. My mind was hungry for more information. I read book after book. Tony Robbins, Jim Rohn, John Maxwell and the list goes on. I read a couple of Dr. Wayne Dyer books, which were right up my alley because I consider myself to be a spiritual person. Being raised by my, God fearing, grandmother introduced me to spirituality at a very early age. I consider myself to be a Christian, but I also believe we are all spiritual beings regardless of our colour, creed or sect, and we are all connected. I finally understood what it meant to have a mind, body and spirit connection. When they are all aligned - one is not complete without the other.

One of the greatest outcomes of being a self-help junkie was being at peace and having my kids see and feel the difference. We were spending so much time together and seeing so much. I was drinking in the beauty of this thing we all call life.

***

The law of attraction was in full force and I was giving birth to new possibilities constantly. God puts things out there for us to have and awaits for our obedience in the form of faith. The kind of faith that lets go of everything, believing without a doubt that everything will work out.

I was in the grocery store when a very tall dark man with a great sense of humour stopped and said, "what are you having for dinner and who are you making dinner for?" He introduced himself as Howard.

"Tuna casserole," I replied, "and it's for me and my two children."

Howard nodded, then reached into his pocket and gave me his business card. "Call me sometime."

"Huh," I said, "yeah right," but I took the card and put it in my wallet.

A couple of weeks later, I found it, and decided "what the hell?" I called him from work.

"Who is this?" he asked.

"Tell me, do you always give your card to strange women in the grocery store?"

Howard laughed. "Ah, that's right! What's your number? I'll call you back later."

Howard was a whirlwind of fun, and somehow I could not believe he was single, but I decided to play along. We talked for several weeks on the phone, at work, or at night after my house work was done and the kids were in bed. I was not giving up the time with the kids for anyone. When he did ask me out, it took about a month to clear my schedule to make it work. Our first date was on his birthday, so I gave him a plant, a card and some Joyce Meyers CDs. From talking with him, I knew he was a Christian.

The time spent with Howard was mind blowing in every way. My prep time to go out with him was days of planning to make sure I looked hot and felt sexy. Howard was so into me and I was beginning to feel like a 25 year old again.

I even introduced him to my family, not as a boyfriend, but just as a friend. Over time, he would come over and hang out with me and the kids, watch movies and play board games and then go home. I wasn't ready to take the next step and I felt something was holding him back too, but I could not put my finger on it.

I expanded my circle of friends to include a beautiful woman and extraordinary friend: Mrs Khan, who worked at the transportation company with me. She eventually started helping me with my children. She was more than a friend; she was like a second grandmother to my children. She was from Bangladesh and a devout Muslim. I loved her and she opened my heart to see that we are all one. We did not see each other as Christian and Muslim women. We experienced one another as friends, mothers and daughters. We enjoyed one another's traditions and cultures. We were Canadian. We were women and because of her my children experienced a grandmother in a way they never had before. The bond that connects us as family is not blood, it is the love, the respect and the trust we hold one another with.

Throughout my life I had on and off experiences with my sister. What she may have never really known is how much I loved her and that I am the mother I am today because of her. She taught me to put children first. I did not look after her because I was forced too. I took care of her all those years because I loved her. She was the peace and smile in some of my roughest days. When Mother would yell at me, Jane's giggle or her cute smile, in her eyes, would make me smile. I learned to become responsible for another life at a young age and that was a real blessing.

In 2009, my sister gave me a journal for my birthday. Inside the cover, she inscribed a note.

"Follow your dreams, they know the way. Let your own story come out. Put something wonderful in the world that wasn't there before. Dare to be your best. Reach beyond your grasp and surround yourself with people who believe you can. Re-define the impossible and know that the best is yet to be. Life is a grand adventure and any life worth living is worth recording. Don't just think it – ink it."

There were several other quotes as well:

What we focus on increases… Rob Estes

When we strive to become better than we are, everything around us becomes better too. Kobi Yamada

It's better to be prepared for an opportunity and not have one, then to have an opportunity and not be prepared; Whitney Young Jr.

To find an open road, have an open mind; John Towne.

One morning, I sat at the kitchen table. The sun hadn't yet come up, and with it being summer, Anton and Sarah were sleeping soundly.

I wrote my first entry.

My vision was continuously discovering forgiveness. To be in a partnership, to raise my children, to build a business and to motivate and encourage others.

I then wrote out a money goal: to make a million dollars and make a difference in the world.

"Today, I begin the process of change. Where I am today: mentally, physically, spiritually, emotionally and financially has to change by me changing the way that I think. One day, someday: happiness starts today, not one day. I forgive myself because I am not a failure as a mother, a friend, girlfriend or daughter. I can ask God for my own forgiveness because I know not what I do. My action and my words have to be in sync in order for me to succeed. I am out of my boat of what stops me. God will do the rest."

I wrote intuitively, with no concern of how it would look to someone else. I gave something deep in my soul a voice on the page. In the months and years to come, I would do the same with one entry after another.

My Journal was my dear diary. A safe place to let go the thoughts in my head, a place of solitude for my heart. Years ago writing these types of things would seem foolish and like a lie . I was a bit of hypocrite. I would pray, say I believe, yet there was some fear in my faith as well. I did not get to know God in an intimate way. One that would have had me feel free of his judgement. God does not judge the faithful. How could He? We are all his children. Now my actions and my thoughts were a match for my prayers. I was one with God.

I recall creating my Seven Decisions for Success:

The buck stops here. I am responsible for my past and my future.

I will seek wisdom. I will be a servant to others in Jesus' name.

I am a person of action. I seize the moment. I choose now.

I have a decided heart.

Today, I choose to be happy. I am a possessor of a grateful spirit.

I will greet this day with a forgiving spirit. I will forgive myself.

I will persist without exception. I am a person of great faith.

And finally, that fall, I decided to do something I'd seen in countless self-help books and seminars: I wrote out the qualities that I wanted in a romantic partner. What the heck! It worked in the Law of Attraction, so let's see if this is going to work for me.

Partnership qualities:

Wants to get married

6ft tall Black male

Age 40-45

No big belly - I do not like big bellies, yet he does not need to have 6 pack abs, yet it would be nice

Financially stable - he has to pay his own bills

Positive mindset

Likes to travel

Gets along with kids

A man of faith

Romantic - enjoys intimacy

A caring lover. LOVES Sex. Lots of it.

Great communicator and patient

Has a sense of humour

We can talk for hours about nothing

Very supportive

Cooks

Is a clean, neat, tidy person

Loves music and can dance

Has his own children but not critical

Believes in growing spiritually

Does not smoke cigarettes or weed

Does not drink alcohol

Will not cheat

A man of his word

He has my back

Creating the list wasn't enough. I embarked on a quest to become the things on the list myself. Everything I wanted in him, I wanted, too, in myself. Next time around, I want to be the Queen of his heart.

All I knew was life was very different. I was able to manage stressful situations without getting sick and overwhelmed or doomed with worry and sleepless nights. As a single mother you can imagine my job and income was vital for my family.

One day, at work, I was called into the HR manager's office. My supervisor was there with a young man who joined the company months earlier. That man was someone who rose to the top very quickly. He said, "Fatima, I'm afraid we have to let you go as part of our restructuring," and went on and on about the usual reasons and regrets that any boss would tell any worker.

I wasn't fazed. I was escorted out of the building gracefully, got into my car and drove off.

The funniest thing happened on my way to work that morning. I was listening to Joyce Meyers. At one point, she said, "if you are on your way to work and you know you are going to lose your job, say this prayer." As I prayed the prayer, I felt comforted, as I knew God would make a way where there was no way. My children would not go hungry and the bills would get paid.

While driving home, I allowed myself a brief moment of breakdown. I felt betrayed. These people at the office had called themselves my "friends," and this was how the treated me.

I was now jobless, but I got into action working on my part-time business and also on getting another job. I was making the effort, but the money was taking its sweet time getting here. With my new mindset, I would have my ups and downs, but I would not give up.

***

In May of 2010 I was invited by a neighbour to go to a record release concert for Echoes of Praise, a local gospel group. That night changed my life. The Pastor's daughter started the prayer and I thought she was talking directly to me. As the group sang, I felt that every note and every line was meant for me.

I left there that night saying to myself, "I must go back to hear what they have to say!"

My journey back to church was an eye opening one. I was on a quest to learn more about God, but I did not want to surround myself with a bunch of religious fanatics. I was always listening with the one ear to hear someone telling us to sell all our belongings and move to Guyana and wait out the 'tribulation'... Can you say: Jim Jones?

The Lead Pastor was not that kind of preacher. He was a teacher in the apostolic tradition. He'd start off with a parable and then connect it to real life. His preaching was very practical and I was able to apply the stories to my life.

I started to notice the funniest thing: I would listen to Joyce Meyer and Joel Osteen before going to church and without the Pastor having any idea what I was listening to before, their messages would align. I often wondered what was going on. Before long, all three messages would align on the same Sunday. Then I knew the universe or God was speaking directly to me. The messages were powerful and moved me into action.

The summer of 2010, the children and I went to Barbados for two weeks. Even though I had no job, my cousin found flights for $55 one way. Peggy put the money on her credit card and I paid her back once I got my income tax money. It was down to the penny. My, did we have an amazing time! I got to spend time with family and friends that I had not seen in 4 to 5 years. I really felt blessed. Everyone took care of my expenses, we had plenty of food to eat and I was on a dream vacation. Could life get any better?

When we returned to Toronto, I stepped off the plane, and noticed there was a message from Howard. He was starting to act very strange and we were on and off. This time he wanted to see me for my birthday. I came back from Barbados because I was volunteering with the Joyce Meyers ministry again, so he was quite lucky to find me again back in the country. We met up and had a great time, but I still could not put my finger on what was up with him.

My neighbour came by one day and was talking about the book she was reading, by Steve Harvey, "Act Like a Lady, Think Like a Man." I had to read the book because it seemed like I could find my answers about how men really think about women. I was not disappointed. My biggest takeaway from the book was to know my place in a man's life. Some of the messages were:

Do you get to meet his friends and family within a certain time frame?

Do you get to meet his co-workers?

Does he open the door for you on dates?

Do you spend time at his apartment?

Is he fishing or is he serious about you?

Ask the question: how does he feel about you?

Ask the question: what does he think about you?

I had my smoking gun for Howard and was ready to shoot the next time I saw him.

On that next occasion we had dinner at his house and, afterward, spent our time watching TV. I told him about the book I was reading.

"Oh yeah?" he said, sounding very defensive. I thought it was something to do with the book, so I let it go.

Later on, in a moment of intimacy, I asked him, "what do you think about me?"

"Oh," he replied, "well, you're a great person, a wonderful mom and lots of fun to hang out with."

"Once," I said, "you said you were just as happy being at my home eating bagels and oatmeal."

"Yes," he replied, and smiled, "I love those kinds of times with you."

Okay, a voice said in my mind, go in for the kill and ask him what you really want to ask him.

"So, how do you feel about me?"

There was a two-minute pause. My heart stopped. "Howard, how do you feel about me?" He said nothing still and I got annoyed. "Look, you've already answered that I'm a great person, but Steve Harvey says these are two different questions with two different answers."

Howard got mad. "Who the hell cares what Steve Harvey says? Why are you trying to analyze me?"

Silence. I didn't know how to respond. I was angry and felt betrayed because here in this intimate moment, I had let him in and this is how he was answering me? So my mind went to the other thing I wanted to ask.

"Is there someone else?"

Another pause. My God, he was just killing me that night!

"Howard?"

Howard sighed. "I'm engaged."

What the hell?!?

I started to yell, scream and hit him with my fists. Amid all the tears I asked, "where has she been for the past nine months?"

"We broke up just before you and I met," he said. "But now she wants to get back together and my parents are pressuring me to get married. She's my logical choice."

See how easy that was for him? No one knew about me and I was never a consideration since I had two children already. Wow!

I left that day so hurt and broken. When I composed myself, I gave myself 24 hours to feel what I needed to feel, to cry, be disappointed and be angry. At the end, I would pick myself up and come up with a new plan of action. To deny my feelings would be nuts and would result in me carrying it around for life.

Within 24 hours, I was good and ready to move on. The plan was to stop dating, seek God more, look for a job and spend time with my children. This was the first time since they were born that I had so much time with them. I was able to make them breakfast and lunch, walk them to school and pick them up. This time of bonding was amazing.

As for Howard, he called every once in awhile, but I didn't have much to say. He came by my house one day to start up where we left off. I took one look at the wedding ring on his finger and started to push him. "I rebuke you in the name of Jesus!" I said to him. He looked at me like I was crazy, did not say much and left.

***

One Sunday after we returned home from our trip, I heard a message about being married and how God made Adam a helper by creating Eve. I realized how I, too, should have a helper and how I deserved to be loved, no matter what happened to me in the past. I left church that day praying for a helper and just as I had discovered the transformational program that altered my life and made me realize that I am the possibility of love and to be loved, I started asking "why not me?"

Christmas holidays were coming up, the year that Howard and I stopped dating, and life was good. I was sitting at home one night. There was no snow outside. God was in His heaven and all was right with the world. And as I got to thinking, there he was, he popped in my head again. It was Ron. "I wonder what happened to Ronald Gould?"

I would replay the last time I saw him with that girl at the Eaton Center food court. They looked like they were so much in love, looking into each other's eyes and laughing. I felt so sad like I lost a past love that I would never get back.

Something came over me and I decided to look him up on Facebook. A co-worker encouraged me to create an account, as it was a great place to connect with people from your past. I had tried, over the years, to find him and he never came up.

It was New Year's Eve and I went to church. I had a few moments to myself before everything started up. I closed my eyes and started a conversation with God. "Okay," I said, "you know what, God? I'm going to stop with the dating, all of it. Whoever it is that you send, I'll be okay with him. If I take two years to get him, I'm okay with that. I'm just going to be by myself and have no relationship." I opened my eyes and waited for the service to begin.

The Pastor began the service and invited everyone to take out a paper and pen and list every goal that we wanted God's help in achieving and how we wanted the year to shape up. It could be anything that mattered to us: relationships, health, wealth, community and the world.

On my piece of paper, I wrote out several different goals and dreams. At the end of it, I wrote one concluding sentence:

"To be married."

I looked at the words for a moment, folded the letter and then put it in the envelope.

Wait, I then thought: no, I don't really want to be married.

I took the letter out and unfolded it, hovered the pen over the line to cross it out... but my hand didn't move. "No," I said out loud, "just send it as it is." I folded the paper back into the envelope and before I could doubt myself again, sealed the envelope and handed it in.

A few weeks later, it was January 13th, and I was listening in on an online training session for my marketing business. "As an agent, you can reach out to people all over the world to build your team. We're not limited by national boundaries and you shouldn't be, either.

Hmmm, I thought, I wonder if Ron would be a good contact. He's somewhere out there in the world. A few seconds later, I thought: no, probably a waste of time. I had already checked before Christmas. He's not there.

That's when a familiar little voice appeared in my head. "Go look right now."

I sighed. I went to Facebook and logged in and then I typed his name into the search field. Again, all the Ronald Goulds' of the world popped up... along with a new profile I hadn't seen before. It was sideways for some reason, so I tilted my head to see the face. I saw that cool expression and mischievous hint of a grin and I knew. There he is!

My finger could not click the mouse fast enough to hit the "Add Friend" button. I went to the bathroom and then came back five minutes later. He'd accepted my request! I clicked on his profile. Ron was living in a place called Melbourne, Florida, close to Orlando. My stomach sank. He's all the way there? Good luck with that nonsense.

Still, it couldn't hurt to send him a message.

"Hey Ron, how are you, do you remember me, it's Fatima from Bloordale?" I typed out.

Within a few seconds, he answered back. "I'm great! Long time no see! How are you and of course I remember you?"

I went to type some more, but I found the whole thing unwieldy. "Listen," I typed after a few exchanges, "I can't talk this way. What's your phone number?"

He sent it to me, and before long, I was calling him in Florida. When he picked up the phone, I heard his voice. It was deeper than I had remembered it and heavier in the sense that this was someone who had lived a few more years than the boy I had last seen.

"I was worried you wouldn't remember me," I told him.

"Of course I did," he replied. "Who could forget that kiss?"

I blushed and laughed. "You liked that, huh?"

Ron laughed. It was such a good sound to hear. "That was the best kiss I ever had in my whole life. Do you remember it?"

"Of course I do!"

We talked late into the night, about three hours. "You'll never believe who I got married and had kids with," he said.

"Who Stacie Clark?"

"Remember the last time we saw each other in real life?"

I thought back to the Eaton Centre when I last saw them together.

"Wasn't that our old friend Stacie from high school?"

"It was," said Ron.

"Oh my God!"

"I know, right? I'm still pissed."

The anger in his voice caught me a little off guard. Ron was still upset over how that had all ended up. After some more cussing and cursing, we changed topics and continued on. That's when I thought about Carlin, and how for all of the badness that had happened, I no longer resented him. He was the children's father and nothing bad had happened since our last chat two years earlier.

Eventually, we got tired. "Listen," I said, "you have to go to work in the morning, we will talk soon.

"Sure," said Ron.

"Well… okay then, have a good night! Talk to you soon"

"Of course," said Ron. "Good night."

***

I realized the next day I had not gotten Ron's email address to keep in touch with him, so I called him back with that purpose in mind.

"Hey," he said when he picked up the call, "you're calling back!"

"Yes I am," I replied, and Ron laughed that deep, heavy laugh that was so good to listen to. "I called to get your email address so we can stay in touch."

Too bad he lives so far away, I thought. I would love to stay in touch with him as a friend. Long distance romances aren't my thing.

"Well, what's the best way I can stay in touch with you?" asked Ron.

"Oh, you can call me. I don't want to run up my phone bill."

He laughed and said, "Fair enough. I'll call you every day until you're sick of me."

I never got sick of talking to him. And he taught me how to use Google Phone from my laptop, so it cost me nothing to speak to him.

I learned how much he had gone through. He talked about his relationship with Stacie because he was really angry with that, how he was in the states but he wasn't there permanently and had never gotten his green card. He talked about his music and what good musicians his sons were. Our children were around the same age, which was nice. The more I listened, the more I saw that Ron's life, like mine, had not turned out the way he had planned. He'd gone through quite a lot of shit, too, and now he was getting older and feeling the same hand of time on his bones as I was on mine.

Ron's cussing was a problem before too long. "You know," I said to him at one point, "I'm not going to talk to you if you keep swearing because it's really getting on my nerves." Immediately, he stopped.

Every time we were about to hang up, Ron would say, "I have very strong feelings for you." I didn't know what he meant by that. "Okay, sure," I would say, right before saying "Bye!""

For nearly a month, that's how things went. Then Valentine's Day was rolling around in my day planner. I was about to call Ron again and the little voice spoke up again in my head.

"You should tell him that you love him."

I frowned. "Oh really?" I said out loud in the car. It was way too soon. Four weeks to tell somebody you haven't seen, in 25 years, that you're in love with them? Ridiculous. I should wait six months to a year.

At the end of that night's call, though, I found the feeling was there, but before I could say it, that old protective part of me just jumped up. Ron was still saying something, but I wasn't hearing it over the screams of my learned instincts. Images of Carlin, of being shoved and pushed into a closet door while carrying a child, of being sold out by my own Mother when I called her for help and a hundred other bad memories of betrayal and heartbreak all flashed through my awareness. The voice spoke again, not the quiet divinity that had led me to look for Ron, but my own identity saying, "girl, if you let those words leave your lips now, you will regret it forever."

"I'll talk to you later, Fatima," said Ron. Shit! It was now or never! I ignored the screaming in my head and summoned my courage.

"I'll talk to you later, then," I said, then paused before adding, "I love you."

And Ron said, without flinching. "I love you too."

Oh my God. He loves me! Yes, he loves me. My face swelled up with emotion, my heart was racing so fast and the feeling of butterflies filled my tummy; the same ones I felt in the hallway years ago, fluttered around my stomach. It was like we had a moment again in time! It was interrupted for us both to go through life and we were now continuing where we left off.

"Yeah," said Ron. "That's what I've meant all this time when I end the call saying I have strong feelings for you."

We hung up, and I leaned back against the chair with the phone in hand, smiling.

After all this time, Ronald Gould loves me.

Later that night, a deliveryman came around trying to find me. He had a bouquet of flowers Ron had ordered for me, all the way from Melbourne, Florida. In the years I had been with the children's father, Carlin had never sent me flowers, not even for Mother's Day. "You're not my mother," he would say on Mother's Day, "so I don't need to give you anything." It was the same thing for my birthday. He'd say, "I don't need a special day to give you anything."

Years of that kind of thing, and yet, only one month into chatting with Ronald Gould, thousands of miles away, and this guy sends me flowers. In that moment, I knew. I wanted him! I needed him! He was the one I asked God for. The question now was where do we go from here?

Super-Fan-Tabulous!

Chapter Thirteen

"Nothing can break apart two hearts that are meant for each other. No distance is too far, no time is too long and no other love can break them apart." I recall reading this quote, years back, by Cat Stevens, and how I put my foot down when it came to men that requested I engage in a long distance relationship. I always responded with a stoic expression on my face as I said, "I don't do that," cutting off any opportunity to even discuss it. And now here we are: Ron and I were separated by thousands of miles, yet I felt more connected to him than I had with anyone I'd ever lain in the same bed with.

He loves me! Ron Gould Loves ME, Fatima, and Fatima Loves Ron! I was thinking we must be crazy. Is this real? We had only been speaking for a month. I closed my eyes. In that moment I heard God speak to me, "Trust me." Yes, of course. That's it! Of course this is real. I asked God for this. God planted the seed in us when we were 12 years old. Our love started then and has been growing ever since. It never stopped. It IS true, nothing can break us apart: not distance, not time nor any other man or woman. God knew us before we were born. He created us to love each other. We needed to grow and experience life, evolve into who we were now, in order to be prepared for one another. When Ron was saying, "I have strong feelings for you," he knew right away what he felt. I did not trust and that was why I didn't understand until I could no longer suppress myself from saying those three words: I love you.

That day, I repeated in my head that 'Ron loves me' I don't know how many times! I know for many it probably seems crazy, but I know my God. He creates what others believe is impossible. Nothing comes easy, but when it arrives, we can either be skeptical or we can embrace it as truth.

Next steps. What will we do next? How will this work? Can we survive this? Yes we can! Besides, I gave my request to God and I was now handing it all over to him. "Thy will will be done." That's it. Heavenly Father, I pray that it is your will that Ron and I be united in love.

My questions got answered only a couple of weeks later.

***

One night when we were speaking, Ron shared with me that he wanted to come back to Toronto to see his mother. He hadn't seen her in 12 years and his mom was having health issues. He confessed that he was torn between being close to his children and worried about his mother.

"Why is that?" I asked.

"Because I don't have a green card. So if I leave the US, I might not be able to return."

Hearing this I couldn't help myself, I went straight into my head. I was anxious and flushed with disappointment. This meant he might not be able to come see me.

Since my transformation, I'd discovered that when I get stuck in my head, nothing gets done. So I chose once again to listen to God and get out of my head. We had several conversations and prior to each one I prayed that God would speak through me so that I wouldn't get triggered. I loved Ron and wanted him to be able to do what was best for him. At this point I questioned if we would be together. With each conversation we grew closer and I was reminded of all those walks home from school. We were like two peas in a pod and we always had so much to discuss. I often thought: Ron loves to hear the sound of his voice and then realized, no. He loves to hear what I have to say too. I liked that.

Then, one night, Ron asked me a question, out of the blue, that changed everything.

I sat there stunned.

"Huh?"

"You heard me," he said after I didn't respond. "I'd really like to marry you."

Did Ron Gould just ask me marry him? If only he could have seen me. My mouth dropped, my eyes were bulging out of my head and my leg started shaking with a vengeance. I closed my eyes and calmness set over me. In that moment, I felt my spirit talk through me.

"Well, I'd like to marry you, too!" Oh my God, what was I saying? I could not believe this was happening and, at the same time, it felt natural. This is what love looks like. Ron had shown me love since I was 12. My hero, the man who stood up to Mother, my first kiss, my great friend, the man I trusted fully and the man that my soul could understand. Yes! I would marry him.

Just like that he said, "How do you want it to look?"

"How do I want what to look?" I asked confused.

"Our wedding?" he said so confidently.

And just like that, we were talking about churches, receptions and colours. Within a few days and several conversations later, we had our entire wedding planned! With every word we exchanged, I had to pinch myself; with every laugh, I felt overwhelmed with Joy. With each word he said, in the sound of his deep voice, all I wanted to do was be with him; smell his essence, touch his skin, have him rest deep inside me, and never come out. We choose July the 8th the following year to be married. Ron would move back to Toronto. This conversation was fun and each day I could not return to Fantasy Land. Deep down, I believed that is all it was: a beautiful fantasy.

So after one of our convos, I had to put on the brakes.

"Okay, all of this is fine, but maybe we should meet up face to face."

"Of course, I would like that."

Before this went any further, I needed to meet him. I needed to know all of this was real. I was going to be in Atlanta again in June and told him I could come and stay with him for a couple of days, and then go to the convention.

"Okay, that sounds great." he said.

Ms. Fatima… you are on your way to see your hero! I booked the flight and before long, I found myself packing my bags. I was as excited and as scared as I could be - all at the same time. I did not have a job and questioned if I was being irresponsible. I was flying to Atlanta in hopes that the part-time marketing business would develop and that I wasn't wasting my money. But money aside, most of all I was scared that I was headed into another life disappointment. My cousin came to pick me up, bags packed, sitting on the steps awaiting his arrival and wow did I look good. Two weeks of preparation, oh man was I ready!

The sound of the voice in my head started to yell at me. What is wrong with you? Why are you going to Florida to see this guy? You haven't seen him in 25 years! Suppose he's a mass murderer? Suppose he kills you, chops you up, stuffs you in garbage bags and buries them in the everglades? What the hell is wrong with you? Where are you going? You need to not get on this plane right now! I started to break down on the stairs and cry. My cousin arrived. A new voice entered my head said, "Get on the plane Fatima." This again was the voice of God, the voice that never led me astray and so I went.

***

I landed in Orlando at 9 o'clock a.m. and it wasn't yet too hot. The air felt like the Caribbean. When I disembarked, there was no one on the platform. I walked out to the driveway, and there were no cars... except for a red one that was approaching. I looked at the driver. Ron?

He parked in front of me and got out of the car. He was wearing a striped shirt and a fedora with no sunglasses. He was looking hot!

"Oh My God... Ron!"

He grinned. "Fatima," he said back.

We approached each other and hugged. Damn, he was buff! I felt his six-pack abs against my body. He wasn't wearing cologne, but he smelled so good! He loaded my bags into the trunk and then got into the car. Just like that, we were drawn into a kiss, that very same kiss. The one that left a tattoo on my heart for over 25 years. The one my soul remembered. It eased my fear instantly. Everything felt right.

"Oh, I want to take you to this older part of Orlando," he said to me. "There's this Vietnamese place that sells these awesome sandwiches." We drove around for an hour in the sunshine, but we couldn't find it. At every red light and stop Ron would turn his head with that slow side turn and kiss me. When we stopped for gas, we got out and just kissed. I had never become so lost in the rapture of a kiss. Kissing him was better than sex. Every inch of my body was filled with these unknown sensations. This is what love feels like. I lusted for every inch of him. The entire day was a blend of holding hands, conversation and our kisses. This is what heaven must feel like and what it felt like to me. My Ron was my heaven. Night-time came along and we went back to where he was staying. The room was nice, very simple, comfortable and safe. We had dinner at an Indian restaurant. I could not help but run wild in my head thinking about what sex would be like with him. I mean if that kiss made my pussy pulse like socca, what on earth would being intimate with him really do to me?

It was getting late, we were tired and just like that something unusual came out of his mouth.

"Look, I'm not ready for anything sexual right now. I want to be up front about it."

"Really?" I said.

"I don't have sex with women I don't know all that well." I was taken aback as I did not understand that. I mean he knows me. He knows me well, but I stopped and allowed myself to be with what he'd said. We just had the most beautiful day and I did not want to ruin it. Besides, intimacy is what I asked for, it was right there on my list and I got it. We slept in the same bed and he just hugged me all night long.

The next day we went to the beach. I was coming out of the water that had been rough and twisted my wrist. I was not sure what was wrong but it hurt. Ron bought me a sling for it, but I couldn't shower myself or carry anything.

We got home that night and I needed to shower. "Ron," I said to him, "can you shower me. I can't afford to hurt my hand. I don't have insurance coverage here."

Ron looked at me. We hadn't had sex and we hadn't even undressed in front of each other. Those little anxieties came back for a moment. I was going to be naked in front of this man.

"No problem," he said right away.

I walked over to the bathroom. He stood in front of me. I looked up into his eyes. He looked straight into mine. He started to undress me. His hands touching my bare skin as he removed my clothing. He stared at every part of me with care. The look on his face was like nothing I had ever seen. He caressed me with his eyes. I just stood still there in silence, wondering if he could hear my heartbeat or the heat my body seemed to be generating down there. I wanted to hold my legs together to control it, but my wetness grew. How could I get this excited over him undressing me?

I was naked. He was fully dressed. He told me to get into the shower with his deep sultry voice. He took the washcloth and soaked it in water. He washed me slowly. He cleaned me with such ease, confidence and respect. This was better than foreplay.

"Man," I said, "you're washing me better than I wash myself."

"Shhh!" he said and kept going.

I said nothing and let him do his thing. After the shower he would cream my entire body and dress me. He repeated this daily until I had to go to Atlanta. One time Ron had to go take a shower. I left the room to go get something from the car and when I returned, I accidentally walked in on him without his towel. I forgot that he was a little whiter than I was. It was the cutest, whitest butt I had ever seen on a black man! He took such good care of me; the kind of man that would make a great partner. He could cook, he was HOT and he could bathe me better than I could bathe myself.

Our time was up and I had to go to Atlanta. He drove me to the airport. My heart was heavy and I could tell how subdued he was. We stood at the check-in counter and Ron took my face in his hands and kissed me for the longest time. We did not care who was there. We could not let go. I wanted him to implant himself in me for the rest of our lifetime.

We slowly stopped. He looked deep into my eyes and said, "I love you."

"I love you," I said back. We let one another go.

I made my way through the crowded line, looking back. Ron was standing there, watching me go. I reached the next counter and he was no longer in sight.

I was on the plane. Was all this true? We did not even have sex, but that was one of the most intimate, precious moments of my life. It felt so right. I knew I needed him with me. I didn't blame him for his circumstances. Maybe it was his fault, maybe it wasn't. Either way that's life, but trust in God and anything is possible. My sadness and longing for him soon turned into excitement. Ronald Gould had promised to marry me and I knew he would keep his word.

I was in Atlanta, feeling high. I looked in the mirror and remembered my last trip there on my 40th birthday. I spoke to God and said I did not want my next 10 years to be like my last. Here I was, 3 years later, Ron had asked me to marry him and I had said yes!

When I returned home, I had to deal with the stress of not having a job and that meant the stress of putting my house up for sale. I had countless interviews and I was living off my savings. I had spoken to my mother about her buying the house, then renting it back to me and me eventually buying it back from her. She would pay the asking price, I would make money on the house and I would give her back her down payment.

However, after the house went up for sale, I called her to ask if she was going to continue with the deal. "No," she said, "this is too much of a risk and I don't want to do it anymore." I wish I could say I was surprised, but I was not. With Mother, I was always waiting for the other shoe to drop.

By August, I was looking for any type of work. My real estate agent gave me a minimum wage job, as his assistant, for 4 hours a day, getting paid bi-weekly. It wasn't much, but it was something to buy food with. By this time, I had already withdrawn my final $5000 from my RRSP. My faith was strong and I continued to go to church and pay my bills.

Ron and I spoke every day online. He was in my corner and offered me money, but I needed *way* more than he could afford. Still though, the gesture was a great one and drew me closer to him.

Within a week of putting the house up for sale I got an offer and I was considering it, but within two days, the couple withdrew. Soon, it was September and I was two payments behind.

I was going through a hard time financially, but my spirit was strong and Ron gave me so much joy. People began to show up for me. My friend and surrogate mother, Ms. Khan, offered the children and I a place to stay once the house was sold. "I love you, Fatima," she told me, "and I'm praying that you find a nice husband to look after you and the kids."

Words cannot express how much I loved Ms. Khan. She was a great friend and a second mom. I remembered the days she babysat my children, driving them to school and picking them up, feeding me when I was sick and including us in her religious celebrations. She was the most amazing cook: the smells that filled her home made my mouth water, my taste buds dance and my belly laugh with satisfaction.

One summer day, I made a date with her to show me how to cook shrimp, one of my favourite things to eat. We started with frying the onions and then preparing the sauce with milk and yogurt. The smells and the aroma that filled the house were breathtaking. We talked about her relationship with her husband and how dedicated she was to her marriage, even though at times he was not good to her. "It's not about him as much as it's about pleasing God, and doing what's right in the sight of God," she said. She remembered what life was like when she met him as a freedom fighter for their country and his cause became her cause. How they come to Canada running for their lives. She left her family behind to follow him and start a family of their own. "God is always watching over me," she said. I asked about her religion and how come she called him God if she is Muslim and why she did not call him "Allah." She told me they're one and the same being, except Christians call him God, but we both believe in the same God. I believed her because she and I were kindred spirits just loving people and humanity.

My Pastor's wife supported me in getting money from the church's 'Loving Kindness' ministry. I got back exactly as much money as I had tithed over the past year when I first lost my job. I had to say: look how good God is! It was at that moment that I got present to how important it is to give God the first fruits of your Labour.

When I thought things couldn't get any worse, my car broke down, with a bill of $500 to fix. I had a good college friend named James who offered to pay to get it fixed. Thank God for His tender mercies. It was during this time that I began writing a gratitude journal. No matter how much life threw my way, I was covered in blessings. I recorded everything no matter how great or how small, to me, they all made a huge difference. I was making a point of celebrating the community of people who loved and supported me.

Regardless of my circumstances, Ron and I continued to a plan our wedding. I was going to use some of the money from the sale of the house and get married, in Florida, so Lionel and Kenny, Ron's sons, could attend. The new plan involved getting married on October 8, 2011 and then he would come to Toronto with me, but those plans changed weekly as no offers came in and no job transpired. We discussed many options including me moving to Florida.

I remember the day in September when I went to tell my mother my big plans.

"Mother. I would like to borrow $3,000 to tie me over until the house sells."

Mother thought about it for a moment then nodded. "Yes, I can do that." I offered to pay back the money from the sale of the house.

"Thank you! Now, I should let you know what the wedding plans will be..." I went over the plan to move to Florida and she gave me a skeptical look.

"Hmmm… are you sure about this man? What about his ex-wife, his kids? Are you sure they won't cause you trouble later on?" It was a pointed question and I understood why she would ask.

"They're good," I replied.

"Okay… well, it's a bit too short notice for me to head down to Florida. I don't know if I'll make it, but if you want, I can watch the kids here while you get settled."

I smiled. "Thank you, but that won't be necessary."

No way in hell am I going to do to them what you did to me, I thought to myself. They were mine and we're all on this journey together. I left the meeting feeling satisfied and much happier than I thought I would be.

***

As the weeks went by, people made appointments to see the house, but no offers.

I was excited about the wedding. My friend Sophie who lived in New York was planning to move to Florida and was going to be my matron of honour. I had called the Florida family court to investigate what we would have to do the get married there. We just needed to apply for the licence. Ron was also going to a church on a regularly basis so we could have a church wedding. The plans were coming together nicely.

I was still sending out resumes and by this time my pastor's wife was calling in favours to get my resume out there. I had a lot of support from her every day and it was shocking to me that she took that kind of interest in my family and me. In the past, I had never been able to talk to my pastors, never mind had their wives call me. I was very impressed by her. Over the coming months, she was one of the people who helped me to overcome several walls.

October came and still, the house wasn't sold. I was starting to panic: unless we sold the house, I had to cancel the wedding in Florida.

"That's fine," said Ron when I told him the bad news. "We can just sell the house when I move back in 2012. It's okay." I was happy he was fine with it, but my heart sank anyway. No tropical wedding.

I started to pray for someone to buy the house and I would have the option to rent the home from the buyer. Being in the real estate office, this option became very real to me. I was speaking to one of the agents, in the office, and he had commented that he owns rental properties.

With hopes of a tropical wedding off the table, I began to focus on getting a job and keeping my children from worrying. My children did not want to leave the only home they knew. Sarah was not having it at all. That was another reason why renting back the home was a good option. I would not have to take them away from their friends and school. I was getting a little more money and the bills were just getting paid. But going to church, listening to Joyce Meyer, Joel Osteen and Creflo Dollar, was what was keeping my faith intact. I believed that the right person was going to buy the house and I would be able to rent it back.

At this time, I was not hearing much from my mother and sister, though I was not surprised. However, I had daily calls from Ron, Sophie and my Pastor's wife. They were the people that God sent to keep me believing. I was reading the Bible daily and also praying and fasting for the first week of every month.

The mortgage was going to be overdue that November because the money I borrowed from my mother was running out. Though I didn't admit it to her, I was devastated when she did not buy the house because all my worries would have been gone. I felt I could not count on her for anything.

"All these years," I said to Ron on the phone one night in October, "and I still can't believe she treats me this way."

"Well," he said, "why don't you tell her? Get it off your chest?"

It seemed like a good idea, so I called her up the next day and asked her. What a mistake that was.

"What I've done to you?" she said, "You slap me in the face by getting married without me and you want to talk about how I treat you?"

"The wedding in Florida's off," I said, " so you don't need to worry about that. We're getting married here."

Then Mother shocked me and started to cry on the phone. All these years, I had never seen or heard her cry. My first thought was that this was some new level of manipulation.

"Mother," I said, "you've given me many slaps in the face over my lifetime. You didn't wait for me to arrive, at the church, when you got married to Clyde, and that didn't seem to be a big deal for you. You still went through with it. That was a slap. After you got married, I felt like the maid of the house, cooking and cleaning up after him before you got home. That was a slap. And remember what you said on the phone when I called you for help with Carlin, when you thought you'd put me on hold? Do you remember those things?"

There was a pause before she said "yes."

I was relieved that the conversation had taken place, but she took it to mean that I had no idea about anything. Afterwards, she stopped speaking to me. My sister, also, stopped talking to me not long after.

Fine! I decided. I didn't need her or any of my family to be part of my life or my wedding! Screw them all! Ignorant Fatima was back in the house!

***

By mid-October, one of the real estate agents, in the office, decided to come by and look at the house as an investment property. When he did, he was very impressed and made an offer. We signed the deal and I was able to rent it back for at least a year.

That was good news, but I still couldn't find work. Around the same time, an agency called saying that a bank was interested in seeing my resume. It was a promising new prospect, but two weeks later, the head-hunter called back to say they changed their mind.

Ron was still talking about moving back to Toronto, but didn't make any firm plans. I was still praying that he would keep his word. Everything was falling apart, but I worked hard to commit to my faith.

I had caught a break with the closing of the house because I no longer had to pay the mortgage, then the closing of the house came, and I went to pick up the cheque from the lawyer. The deductions included their money, plus the penalty for breaking the mortgage and lawyer fees. What's more, the agent who bought the house got a commission plus first and last month's rent, then my real estate agent, and now boss made over $11,000 for the sale of the house. After all those deductions, it left me with a cheque for $16,000. I was angry, upset, lost and crying out in pain. I wondered what God was doing to me and what lesson I was learning. I just did not trust anyone. I only had Ron, Sophie and the Pastor's wife.

I got in my car and drove away in a cloud of tears. I was listening to a CD by Echoes of Praise; a track sung by my Pastor's children called, "Tis So Sweet." Hearing the pastor's daughter singing, "he's got you, he will never leave you or forsake you." Those words kept replaying over and over in my head.

I allowed myself 24 hours to go through what I needed to: disappointment, anger, denial and then acceptance. I did not have to work the next day for the agent, but afterwards, he had the nerve to call me and lecture me about not showing up. I wanted to take my car and run him over or shoot him. He had no idea how upset I was. I owed my mother $3000, I had to put aside rent of $1400 for two months and pay off the credit cards, and other outstanding bills. This left me with $4000 to live off of until I got a job. Not to mention Christmas and my daughter's birthday we're coming.

By the next day, I pulled myself together and came up with a plan. I was going to keep looking for a job by sending out more resumes. In the meantime, I'd keep going to work for a man I wanted to punch the shit out of, but I would keep going.

***

With every hit of hardship, I punched back with my faith. I knew my God would not forsake me. This I knew.

The times I filled up with anger and frustration, the sound of Ron's voice played like music for my heart. He calmed me right down. He got me. This man was so far away, but knew me better than any other man ever had and we still hadn't had sex.

Just like that, Ron and I were discussing him coming to Toronto. Yes! He was coming!

"I can come to Florida to help you move," I told him, "and we'll drive back to Toronto."

"We should do it for the first weekend in December," he said, "before the snow falls."

By this time I had my wedding dress and my rings, but with no date of when I would use them.

Mrs. Khan, the Pastor's wife and Sophie were the angels God put in my life to shine the light in. Like the song, "Tis So Sweet" and in the Bible it said: God would never leave you or forsake you, He gave those three women His Spirit to be with me through this hellish time, to get me over the wall.

I spent the next two months doing part-time jobs from 6 a.m. to 1 p.m. and, in the afternoons, going on job interviews and praying everything would work out. I kept writing in my gratitude journal every day and sending out positive vibes to the universe.

***

The weekend came to go and help Ron move back home.

We were both very excited! I had told the kids he was going to stay with his mother if there was room for him. If not, he was going to stay with us. There was no clear plan: instead, we were going with the flow. I had started talking to friends about getting him a job as soon as possible. "I can cover your expenses until you get a job," I told him, "but I can't be responsible for supporting your children. You'll have to work that out with your kids and your ex-wife." Ron agreed.

I hopped on that plane, in Buffalo, and landed to the warmth of Florida's breezes. God, it was good to be back in that amazing weather! Walking back to the drop-zone in the airport, there was Ron in his car, smiling that bright grin beneath his sunglasses and looking as good as ever! I walked over to him, he kissed me and I returned to heaven! All the days apart were worth the pain just for that one kiss.

We didn't have much time to waste to get everything together. Ron took me back to his place where I met his roommate who was going away for the weekend. We went out for dinner and hung out, just talking about everything and enjoying each other's company. The next day, I was going to meet his boys and have dinner with them.

That night as we lay in his bed, I did not know what to expect. I mean perhaps he was waiting for us to get married before we have sex? In that moment, Ron kissed me. It felt so right to be back in his arms.

His lips met mine. Everything was happening in slow motion and the lust was building. I wanted to take our time in that moment. He put his tongue on me. We were deep into one another. He knew my body as if he had memorized every inch of it when he bathed me. The passion was heavy, the intensity riveting and this sweet loving opened me up in ways I had never experienced before. He was and is everything I needed. My juices were flowing and I was like a virgin in this type of sexual healing. The fire in us was unleashed and he found his way inside me, we were joined as one and I never wanted to be apart again. That kiss turned into hours of lovemaking and ooohhhh my, was this man damn good and so worth the wait! Ron was the perfect blend of super and fabulous. I know of no words that could ever describe the sensations and intensity of the orgasms that exploded inside me; so I made one up: superfantabulous! My insides were screaming **'SUPERFANTABULOUS'!**

Yes, I Do

Chapter Fourteen

Pinch me! This was too good to be true! Or was it? This is what life looks like when you hand everything over to God. Time after time, God has proven to have my back and that it is my faith, which got me over all those walls. We cannot live a life problem free, yet we can live a life free from the torture of self-doubt, suffering and fear. It takes time, yet it is possible. Faith feeds hope and hope feeds life. Hope is the anchor that banishes hopelessness and for that reason we actually have a choice in how life will unfold for us. With every tear and cry for help, I grew. I had evolved into this woman who allowed herself to trust her choices and love this man named Ron. The love of my life!

The first time I saw his face, I saw myself and the first time he kissed my lips, my world was forever shaken. I had a glimpse of love and now true love had finally found me. I put this out into the universe and the universe spoke back to me. My heart was alive with happiness and once again there was God answering my prayers.

Ron was more than I could have hoped or asked God for. Once again, God had not left me or forsaken me. We spent a day hanging out with his boys, Kenny and Lionel. Ron made us all dinner and we spent the time together talking. The next day we rented a car. We dropped off his old car to his ex-wife's house so she could sell it and keep the money. We also said goodbye to the boys and drove around the city to say goodbye to his old friends. Our last stop was in Orlando to say goodbye to the couple Ron had lived and worked with for years.

A new chapter in both our lives were about to begin. We drove off into the sunset and for the next 17 hours we listened to inspirational and spiritual CDs, and enjoyed the peace of our silence as we held hands and exchanged mental energy.

"I can't wait to see your house," Ron said, a little tired from the road.

"You will," I said, "but first, we're going to see your mother."

By the time we pulled up to his mother's house in Toronto, his sister was outside at the door to greet him. I was taken aback! They had been sitting and waiting for us to show up. Mrs. Gould was an old wrinkled white woman who clearly loved her son. Once inside, Ron's mother just hugged him, kissed his face and told him how much she loved him. I stood there with my eyes watering and my heart full.

We got to see some of the things Ron had when he last lived here and things she had been keeping for him. A lot of black memorabilia she had gathered to honour Ron's black heritage and to pass on to her grandchildren. His sisters gave him a box of old childhood memories. I was quite amazed at how this white woman, who had four children of her own, had adopted and mothered a mixed child. My heart went out to her and I respected her for adopting a child of a different race.

It was also at that moment that I got present to the goodness of God in Ron's life. I saw how he and his family loved music, art and historical literature. So much of him was a part of that family. It was an amazing moment in our relationship! We took a lot of pictures that night of Ron's homecoming and his reunion with his mother. He had left a young man and come back a full-grown man with children. At that time, we also realized he could not stay there. The house was a hoarder home. Every room was taken up with mountains of paper, books and all kinds stuff.

Once we got into the car, Ron broke down and cried. It was very emotional for us both. All I could do was to comfort and reassure him that he had made the right decision to come back before something happened to his mom and he would never forgive himself. The time spent away from his children could be made up, but the time with his mother was precious. We got back on the road to my house.

Three days later, his mother went into a home and that night of his homecoming was the most lucid she would be in the months to come.

I was so happy for Ron. He got to spend precious time with his mother. Over the next several months he visited her, played the guitar for her and wrote her a song. I was very proud of him. I too went along with my children to visit her in the home. I enjoyed the rare moments when Patricia Gould would remember her son; however, those times became fewer and fewer making it difficult for him to endure the visits emotionally, but I still encouraged him.

At that moment, I realized my life was about to change drastically and I had not prepared my children properly for what was about to happen to them. My daughter was my biggest concern because she did not accept changes too well.

Within two weeks of Ron's home coming, he had his first job at a place that sold restaurant equipment. He was paid minimum wage. Life, at home, was becoming difficult because my children were not prepared properly. There was resistance from the kids. My daughter wanted back her place in my bed, sleeping with me on Friday and Saturday nights was our custom, but her spot was taken by Ron. There were a lot of shouting matches and I fought hard to avoid taking sides.

Once again, the Pastor's wife came to help me. "You must let your children know that you'll always love them," she said, "and that 'now you are going to have a husband and he also has a place in our house.' Tell that soon, they will be all grown up and leaving…" I took her advice and prepared the children for Ron's long-term stay. The transition was very hard on me, because I loved them all, and I wanted them all in my life. I did my best to accommodate everyone. It took to a lot of prayer.

During this time, the church was going through a name change. I called my Pastor and told him we wanted to be the first couple to be married under the new name. The Pastor and his wife were some of the first people I introduced him to. The Pastor's wife seemed very pleased and she made it her mission to find him a job. She told me we would have to make an appointment with the Pastor about the wedding.

At that meeting, we decided the wedding would be on Sunday January 1, 2012 and that would give us two weeks to plan and get everything ready. Wow! That was going to be very quick.

The Pastor's wife guided me every step of the way. Again, God's angels' light was shining in my life.

"Who are you going to invite?" she asked. "How many?"

"Ten," I said. She gave me a funny look.

"What?"

"Ten people," I repeated. "I can't afford a $10,000 wedding right now."

"Well," she said, "you should go ask people to contribute to the wedding."

I listened and started asking.

My barber from Barry cut my hair, Ron, and Anton's hair as a wedding present. My friend, Nevelyn did my daughter's hair as her gift. My sister was my matron of honour and she had a dress to wear in her closet. Her dress was black and the theme became black and white. During the planning, we learned that Ron's sons wouldn't be able to make it, which was upsetting to Ron, but we pressed on. My daughter had a white dress from her grade five graduation that she had not worn yet. I had to buy my son some black pants and a vest to go over his white shirt. We would wait for Boxing Day sales at the jewellery exchange downtown to buy his ring and get it for a good price. We were resourceful, despite our lack of resources, and it was paying off.

One Friday, we drove to City Hall to get the marriage licence. When we talked to the clerk, all of our positive vibes came crashing down. "Ron's divorce was in the US," the clerk said, "so you'll need to provide proof of that from the State of Florida and then apply to Thunder Bay. We can't just grant you one here."

The problem was that the following week was Christmas everything was shutting down. We had to hire a lawyer to write a letter to Ron's lawyer in the U.S., because Ron did not have his official divorce papers. The lawyer would have to send off the application to Thunder Bay.

A lot of prayers went out for the licence to come back in time.

Meanwhile, the Pastor's wife called every couple of days to see how the plans were going. I got my cousin Toni to make me a shawl to go with my dress. My sister was baking the cake and my cousin Yvonne created the dessert table.

I had invited 40 people to the wedding and the reception was going to be at my home. Ron cooked the food and my cousin's friend came to the house and decorated while we were at the church. My Pastor's wife was right: people were willing to contribute to my big day! My daughter and I created and printed the program using our computer. They were beautiful on black and white paper. I got flowers for my sister, my daughter and myself to carry. They were calla lilies. Mrs. Khan's daughter prepared them for me. We made time to visit Mrs. Khan. She was too sick to attend the wedding, but her daughters came. I was very happy about that.

The Thursday before the wedding, I got a call about picking up the marriage licence. Once again I had to give God all the glory. The Pastor gave us premarital counselling. Now that was something! Both Ron and I answered the first questionnaire with all the same answers. I gave God thanks, at that time, for the long distance relationship and the many hours talking on the phone about the past, present and the future of our lives.

It was during one of those sessions that the Pastor asked if my mother was coming. "I don't know," was my reply. "You should have a conversation with her," he advised me. "Just tell her your plans and request her presence there. Don't ask her permission. It's an invitation, not a request."

When I called her not long after that conversation, I got Clyde, my stepfather, on the phone. He seemed very angry with me and I didn't know why.

"I'd like for you to walk down the aisle with my son," I said.

"I don't have any shoes to wear," he replied.

"You can wear anything you'd like from your closet. The wedding isn't going to be formal, so it's not necessary to spend money on new clothes."

"We'll get back to you," he told me. And they never did.

It was not until the wedding rehearsal that I got present to what a big deal it was. Maybe I should have waited until we had the $10,000 to spend.

The children and I went to church for the New Year's Eve service because it was that night in 2010 that I wrote in my letter to God that I wanted to get married. My letter to God was answered. The universe was celebrating our love and one year later I was getting married to the man of my dreams.

***

The moment was here and the wedding was just about to begin. I was waiting for my cue from the song we had chosen and, instead, I heard the sound of a voice singing. There he was, standing, so handsome beside the Pastor. He was singing a song to me as I walked down the aisle. Anton was on my left and Clyde on my right. Could this get any better?

Ron wrote this song just for me and I inhaled every word.

And he sang...

I love her, Yes I do,

I love her, and this love is true,

I've grown weary,

　Clearly,

I don't want anybody new,

I've fallen in love,

And now no one else will do,

I used to hide behind a cloud,

I wouldn't let anybody see,

What was go in' on,

Inside of me,

But then she came along,

And somehow wrestled me out of my keys,

And now I'm changing my whole life,

To accommodate her dreams,

Cause I love her, Yes I do,

And I knew right from the start,

She was a world apart,

From other girls I knew,

And I love her… Yes I do,

I hear the birds singing, in the trees,

I watch the flowers entertain the bees,

I feel a warm, gentle, summer breeze,

And when I look into her eyes it's,

It's my future that I see,

Cause I love her,

Yes I love her… Yes I do,

And I thank heaven above,

For sending me a love, So true,

And I love her, Yes I do,

I knew right from the start,

That we would never part, Cause I'm stuck like glue,

Cause I love her, Yes I do.

The Ceremony began. I had a perma-grin all over my face. I could not believe I was standing in front of this man. The Pastor spoke of love, commitment and God's love. This wedding was a result of it all. The moment came.

"Fatima Devonish do you take Ronald Gould to be your lawfully wedded husband?" Said the Pastor.

"I do," I said so naturally. I had been waiting my entire life to say those two words.

"And do you Ronald Gould, take Fatima Devonish to be your lawfully wedded wife?" The Pastor looked up at him with a beautiful grin.

Ron looked deep into my eyes, his face ever so handsome and said, "I do." I grinned with that sexy smile.

The Pastor proudly stood in front of us all and said, "With the power invested in me by God, I now pronounce you husband and wife, you may kiss the bride."

We leaned into one another and just like that moment at the airport, he pulled me in without a care for who was in the room, and kissed my soul. A kiss so sweet, so true to our love and just like that I was Mrs. Fatima Gould. Thank you God. Oh Heavenly Father. Thank you.

After the ceremony everyone came to our house. The food, the wine, the desserts and the laughter was as if it took a year to plan this. I never wanted it to end. I held on to every moment, silently saying: thank you, thank you, thank you God, over and over in my head. The lights went dim and it was time for our dance. Our wedding would not be complete without returning to that night, so long ago, when two awkward kids first held each other close for everyone to see at a middle school in 1980... **Hey Jude...**

I Am Over The Wall

Epilogue

Hopelessness, is a self created phenomenon derived from fear. Those fears paralyze you from living the life you want. If fear conquered me, I would not have had my dream wedding or my Ron. I would not have my kids, my freedom, my peace of mind and, more than anything, I would not be living my life on my terms. I had every reason not to trust the process and to give into my skepticism based on the reminders of my previous failures. There was evidence all around me and continuous fingers being pointed at me that said, "I told you so." I am an ordinary woman living my life. Yet, with faith I have been able to create extraordinary results. When life would give me every good reason to give up, that is when I became a child of destiny.

Who plans a wedding without going on a first date? I did, because I listened to God. After our wedding, it was the beginning of new life and with that came new problems. We were not strangers to hardship, in fact, we were built for it. After our wedding, we had many issues to face and I came to realize that these are just part of life. This time we were not facing it all alone. We had each other's back.

Prayers were over us. I got a new full-time job and started on January 16th, 2 weeks after our wedding. Sadly Mrs. Khan died that very same day. I felt her angelic presence all around me. She was my guardian angel. Because of her, I do not see the world separated by religion and now believe that religion segregates humanity by having us be slaves to particular belief systems. I was Christian and she was Muslim, yet we were still both women and human. There was no difference between us. We were both spirits living a human experience.

Ron, the kids and I moved into a new home. We continued to have our financial struggles and live paycheque to paycheque. Yet we still had great food on the table and a blessed home. Life still throws me curveballs and every once in awhile that Bajan she devil comes outta me. I could not let go of feeling like a failure for losing the home I owned and for now living in a rental. My pastor and his wife, came to bless our home and made me see that a home is not just 4 walls and its material value, it is the heart of a family. God is everywhere regardless of what the place looks like. That fixed me up real good.

The first summer with all of us together was hard. The transition was difficult for the kids and they could not accept Ron in their home or knowing their mom was married to anyone other than their father. Prayer made its way through all of our spirits. Finally peace came over us. For the longest time it seemed like we were doing this over and over again, yet eventually the kids and Ron became friends.

Having blended families is hard for everyone. This was especially so for Ron seeing as he couldn't always see his children as often as his heart called for them. He is a good father. He taught his boys the art of music and the beauty of the man I love is inside of them both. Life was changing and moving so fast. One summer Ron's kids came to visit us and we were all together. The 4 kids and us had a great time. We were evolving as a family. Ron enrolled in that transformational program that I did. His path to self discovery elevated and our lives. I cannot imagine what it is like for him to be away from his boys, yet we are doing everything we can to ensure they are reunited.

Ron's mother died, but his sons had the chance to see her before she passed. He was able to share with them why he left and all of the children bonded. Ron and I to this day live a life of ups and down, mood swings, arguments, daily stress and everything else that life serves us. We are no different than any other husband and wife. I am certain, in my heart, that I will be with Ron until I am old and gray. It took me 25 years to finally have my moment and

I am going to hold on to it for dear life. Our marriage is a sweet recipe of good food, great conversations, heart pumping sex and unconditional love. The kind of love that has us give up being right even when we know we are right, hold back our judgements, give up pointing the finger and create a life we both love together. He is my best friend and soul mate.

As for the rest of my life, hitting the walls made me stronger. It continues to teach me that when I am blinded by my troubles, faith will allow me to see. I hold the power to get over any wall that stands in my way.

I no longer allow self-righteousness to rule my ways. I have come to the realization that my children's father continues to do the best he can. He never had the opportunities to be free of his past as I have. It is not his time yet and I continue to pray over him. He is a good father. Today, he supports them and they all spend time together. We even talk, regardless of our differences of opinion, as he was an important part of my life. He is the reason why I have my babies and for that reason I will be grateful to him forever.

Throughout the journey of writing this book, I have discovered that the hatred I had for my mother was a lie. How can I hate the person that carried and protected me in her belly for nine months? She kept me alive and gave me to my grandmother because, at the time, it was the only thing she knew. If she didn't do that I would have never known and loved my Ma as I do. Her love has been a blessing for me and I am the woman I am today because I had two mothers. I know now none of this was Mother's fault. Just like the woman before her, that generational curse hovered over my mother. As Christ said, "forgive them, for they know not know what they do."

I am the interruption in the blood line. My children will never experience my pain as I am creating them to be greater human beings. As their mother, I am the first example of love that they would know and I am dedicating my life to showing them what a life looks like when faith leads the way.

True forgiveness is not wishing the past did not happen. It is acknowledging it existed and letting go of what you cannot change. Forgiveness does not make what others have done to you right, it sets you free and that is who I am. I gave up proving why Mother, Carlin and every other person was wrong. Now, I ask God to speak through me and I put myself before him, so that what comes out of my mouth is for the good of others.

This book was a gift to me; one I never expected was going to come my way. I will be honest, it was not easy. It first started with a gathering of some friends and an idea of creating a book that would guide people to take new actions in their lives based on some of my life experiences. Honestly, I wanted to create a booklet that you could keep in your purse or carry in your back pocket. I still laugh everyday about the original plan. Nothing could prepare me with the force of guidance that was headed my way. No one is ever really prepared to meet someone who challenges you to be your best self, to demand you live an extraordinary life and, most of all, give you the courage to tell the truth about your own life story, so that others would be inspired to remove the mask of shame in order to be free.

This book was therapy for my soul. An opportunity to have my life story told through the eyes of another. God sent me this woman, I did not even like when I first met her. I, like many black woman, immediately judged her. "Who does that white woman think she is?" I would say. Yet, the moment we sat down at my kitchen table, I knew I was speaking to my soul sister. She saw something in me that I did not see in myself. She would not allow me to create my "booklet." She inspired me to tell my story by sharing with others with a humble heart. Through the process of hundreds of conversations, uncomfortable questions, moments of anger and unstoppable tears, she pulled me out of the places of darkness that I did not even know I was in.

The experience of creating this book took my marriage to a whole new level; our love has grown deeper and unfolded in ways that have brought us closer now than we ever dreamed of being. "When I do not know what to say, I sing about you," the words I know fall from the lips of my lover. Our home is filled with music, art and creativity and on this journey he wrote me this letter:

My Dearest Fatima,

You are my lover and my best friend. Gifts like you are as rare as they are precious. Without your doting and preening and constant encouragement I don't know what I'd do. There's just so much love in your heart! No one has ever made me feel more treasured, and as a result, I have never before presented so much of myself as collateral to ensure the object of my desire understands my commitment. It took twenty something years for the Universe to arrange this union and while I wish to God I could turn back time and make it happen sooner. I'm eternally grateful we happened at all. With you in my arms, nothing seems out of reach; nothing seems impossible! And while I've forgotten the details of what it was like before you, I do remember a huge cluttered mess left behind by all the ups and downs of love gone wrong in my life. All that seemed to disappear on that first call that led to this wonderful romance. Suddenly I was twelve years old again, chillin' with my bud, dreaming wild dreams and believing the impossible can, and will happen. Willing to do whatever it takes to make you mine. And so here we are. Hand in hand, staring into a future of infinite possibility, in love, in lust, inseparable.

Yours always,

Ron

For the first time in my life I had a group of real girlfriends; the kind that give it to you straight, share your pain and your happiness. They are my soul sisters and my rock. There is not a day that goes by that we don't speak to one another. We do everything together. I love them with all my heart. These women are also my business partners in transforming the world. I call them my tribe. The four pillars of my happiness.

I believe this woman came into my life to prepare me for my bigger purpose; the one that God is revealing to me every day. Her name is Audrey Hlembizky. She wrote my story. I spoke, she wrote. She asked, I answered. Through all the trials and tribulations I know God sent her to me to interrupt my insecurities, my trust issues and everything else that would stop me from being the greatest version of myself. Regardless, if one or one million people read this book, I am at peace that I had the courage to do this.

My life is a love story and now it is out there for the world to read. I am free and lost inside the blessing of gratefulness. I believe God is using me as a demonstration of what it looks like to remove our limiting beliefs. Divine timing and guidance is key in understanding what steps we are to take to pursue our purpose. Wherever you are right now in your life, you are there for a reason. With time you will see life unfold in a way that reveals one gift after another. When you see life through the filter of your spirit and give up needing to know how or why, life will release miracles. Believe and it will happen. I am you and you are me. When we give up any shame of our past and forgive those who hurt us, especially ourselves, we can go out there, hold our heads up high and share our own stories in order to unleash our faith, freedom and fearlessness, declaring **"I AM *over the wall.*"**

Acknowledgements

To my heavenly Father. God you made me and you placed before me all that you knew I needed to experience so I could be the woman I am today. You continue to guide me so that I may do your work and I am grateful for the gift of my life.

My children, you are my greatest joy and blessing from God. May your lives be surrounded by God's protection and I thank God everyday that I am your mother. My life is complete because of your love. You bring joy and pleasure to my life.

Ron, my husband, we are an example of divine timing. Twenty-five years in the making; I praise God that you never got away. After our first kiss we had the chance to develop into who we became so that when our souls were ready to reunite we were ready to spend the rest of our lives and beyond together. You are the love of my life.

To my mother, thank you for teaching me strength, responsibility and giving me the gift of knowing Ma in the way I did. I am the woman I am today because my spirit has two homes.

Ma, without you I can't imagine who I would be. At 101 years old, you lived a lifetime serving others and you gave me your love. You were a mother to so many. You are my foundation and I will forever be connected to you in mind, body and soul.

To Walter, my father, we did not have much time together here on earth. Yet, I feel your protection everyday around me through your spirit. The time we did have was filled with many blessed moments and I am grateful, that against all odds, we were able to know each other.

To my sister, I have watched you grow up into a wonderful woman of God; devoted wife, mother and talented gifts. My life was blessed through you. You brought so much joy to my life when I saw darkness, and I would not change a thing. Thank you for being someone I could nurture and love.

To my stepchildren, I have grown to love you like my own. As time goes by I know that our bond, as a family, will be unbreakable. You are both amazing young men. It is my prayer for you that you both walk in the path God has laid before you, using your musical talents to bless the world with songs.

Carlin, no matter what we went through, you gave me the greatest gifts of joy; our children. For many years of my life you were my best friend who kept me grounded. You were my source of encouragement when my world was falling apart around me. Life has taken us down different paths, yet I would not be who I am if you were not part of my journey.

Sophie Hall, my angel, who has been my dearest friend from the age of 16. We have seen each other through life's greatest challenges and have shared our tears along with laughter. Your commitment to our friendship has span decades, countries and I don't know what I would do without you in my life. I pray nothing but God's best for you and your family. I love you…

To the Khan family, you have taught me what it means to see beyond color, beyond religion, beyond race and to see the spirit of the man. You embraced me and my children as if we were connected by blood. Even though you are both now in heaven I will never forget you. You will always be in my heart.

To my spiritual parents, words cannot express how I feel about you both. You picked me up when I fell from grace and placed my feet on solid ground. Your prayers, encouraging words and teachings have been my source to get over the walls. I thank you.

To my soul sisters Audrey, Alanna and Simone. When God put you three in my life I had no idea you would become a part of my mind, body and soul. Your unconditional love has been the wind beneath my wings that has caused me to soar. I pray you stay true to the source of your lives and let God's purpose be your passion.

About The Authors

Fatima Gould

"There is hope for anyone, at anytime, at any age."

Fatima has transformed her life to be a catalyst of hope, inspiring a new path of leadership in the world of personal growth and development. As a Community Ambassador for Change, speaker, author and communication coach, she has taken the lid off what others believe is impossible. She is committed to raising the level of freedom with today's youth, women's groups and bridging the gap between fear and faith, so others discover what it is like to fall in love with life. Today, she leads many projects that are creating sustainable change and creating structures to unite powerful leaders who are a stand for others to give up being a victim of their circumstances and then declare and design their created life.

Audrey Hlembizky

"Witness miracles when you love people even when they do not love themselves."

Audrey's fierce and unstoppable declaration to create a world that works breathes life into every action she takes as she embodies the "be the change" mantra. As a high performance coach, author, brand engineer and dream facilitator, her entrepreneurial spirit, awakens new insight and profound wisdom affording her the ability to connect and captivate the mind, heart and spirit of the lives she touches by leading them into a state of self-discovery and empowering them to live beyond their greatness. Her faith, laser focus and passion for humanitarian endeavours are the driving force behind her philanthropic work today with an immeasurable determination to stand up and be a leading voice for women, an empowering mentor for today's families and youth and a change agent that pours out unconditional love for every human being.

Ronald Gould

"Your hopes and dreams are commercials for the life that awaits you once you stop merely thinking about, and start working with, the innate creativity we all possess."

Ronald's passion to bring music into the lives of others inspires him to celebrate the arts and empower people to use them as a natural form of self-expression. He is a talented song writer, musician, author and music coach committed to empowering others to celebrate the arts as their natural form of self-expression. Through his abilities he is able to bring out people's inner star through the whispers of sound. Ronald is committed to encouraging today's rising youth and future world-class musicians to live their dreams, to know that music can never die, as long as we keep making it, and that a melody can bring peace and harmony to the world.

JOIN THE MOVEMENT

Through the journey of writing this book we believed there was a greater need to bring women together to banish the barriers of shame and create a safe place for everyone to be extraordinary. IamOvertheWall.com is an opportunity to be an active part of a community that uplifts you and gets you over the walls of life. All this has been created by a collection of leaders that raise the bar, empower you to witness your own greatness and provide you with the tools required to discover what miraculous living is all about. Joining the movement will allow you to collaborate with an army of women who are lifting the lid off being 'ordinary' to be that woman who leads her family, her community and the world through your life purpose.

Unleash your faith, freedom and fearlessness and get over the walls that stop you! An on-line destination and community to declare and claim your created life.

www.iamoverthewall.com